PRAISE

"I wish I would have read this when I was a teen. It would have encouraged me to let go and be me. Individuality is crucial in life. This book helps explain why it is so important to stay true to yourself." **Olesya Rulin, Actress--*High School Musical 1, 2, and 3***

☆

"The title of this book says it all. ***Be The Star You Are! for TEENS*** *offers hope to teenagers experiencing the darkest phase of their lives. This is a book to treasure always."* **Michelle Izmaylov, Author of *The Galacteran Legacy: Galaxy Watch***

☆

"When I read a book it has to be like talking to a friend...this is it! Made me smile and surf a bigger wave!" **Bethany Hamilton, Pro Surfer, and Teen Inspiration**

☆

"I think being a teenager has always had its challenges, now maybe more than ever. It may seem hard sometimes to follow our intuition over the crowd, but it's when we feel our best...which is why I'm glad there's a book to help people of all ages realize that joy is more important than status and absolutely no one is better at being you." **Cassidy Freeman, Star of CW's *SMALLVILLE***

☆

"Teen peer pressure is undeniably stressful. In this book, Cynthia Brian provides stories and tools that will help teens honor their individuality and uniqueness while learning to deal with peer pressure in a positive way." **Patty Hansen, Author of *Chicken Soup for the Preteen Soul***

☆

"Discover your purpose, passion, and possibilities as Cynthia Brian offers principles of success and leadership in ***Be the Star You Are! for TEENS****. This book is a positive place to awaken your potential and be great!"* **John Arigoni, President and CEO, Boys and Girls Clubs of Metro Denver**

☆

"Wisdom, wit, and winning in the game called life fill the pages of Cynthia Brian's ***Be the Star You Are! for TEENS****. The perfect gift for teenagers and the adults who love them."* **Bettie and Jennifer Youngs, Authors of the *Taste Berries for Teens* series**

☆

*"****Be the Star You Are! for TEENS*** *is your survival guide for finding your purpose and gifts. Think of it as your teen bible for success. You* ***need*** *this book. Cynthia Brian has been my coaching angel and she'll help you spread your wings to reach for the stars! I am following my dream–you can too!"* **Sarah Marleau, Teen Model, Actor, and Martial Artist**

☆

"Cynthia Brian cares about youth and her book, ***Be the Star You Are! for TEENS*** *is one of the ways that she is committed to making a difference."* **Yasmin Shiraz, Award Winning Author of *Retaliation***

☆

"***Be the Star You Are! for TEENS*** *is an excellent book to help all teens reach their potential! Everyday I see kids who have lost hope in themselves. This book can help them regain it."* **Carol Miloszewski, AP English Teacher, and Student Assistance Program Coordinator**

☆

"Teenagers need a golden ticket for success and they'll find it with Cynthia Brian's book. She's an incredibly inspiring person and this is teen talk that you can walk." **Brendon Burchard, Author of *Life's Golden Ticket***

BE THE STAR YOU ARE!®

FOR TEENS

Simple Gifts for
Living, Loving, Laughing, Learning, and Leading

CYNTHIA BRIAN

New York Times Best Selling Author

NEW YORK

Be the Star You Are!® For Teens

Simple Gifts for Living, Loving, Laughing, Learning, and Leading

Disclaimer: The Publisher and the Author make no representations or warranties with respect to the accuracy or completeness of the contents of this work and specifically disclaim all warranties, including without limitation warranties of fitness for a particular purpose. No warranty may be created or extended by sales or promotional materials. The advice and strategies contained herein may not be suitable for every situation. This work is sold with the understanding that the Publisher is not engaged in rendering legal, accounting, or other professional services. If professional assistance is required, the services of a competent professional person should be sought. Neither the Publisher nor the Author shall be liable for damages arising herefrom. The fact that an organization or website is referred to in this work as a citation and/or a potential source of further information does not mean that the Author or the Publisher endorses the information the organization or website may provide or recommendations it may make. Further, readers should be aware that internet websites listed in this work may have changed or disappeared between when this work was written and when it is read.

ISBN: 978-1-60037-632-0

Library of Congress Control Number: 2009926277

Author cover photo by Norbert Brein Kozakewycz
www.norbertphotography.com
510-595-7962

Author photo with rooster by Ken Rice
www.kenricephoto@aol.com
510-652-1752

MORGAN · JAMES
THE ENTREPRENEURIAL PUBLISHER

Morgan James Publishing, LLC
1225 Franklin Ave., STE 325
Garden City, NY 11530-1693
Toll Free 800-485-4943

www.MorganJamesPublishing.com

Cover Design by: 3 Dog Design
www.3dogdesign.net

Quantity discounts are available for educational, business, charitable, and sales promotions.

Proceeds benefit the charity, Be the Star You Are!®, a 501 c3 empowering women, families, and youth through improved literacy and positive messages.

P.O. Box 376,
Moraga, California, 94556
www.bethestaryouare.org
877-944-STAR (7827)

Habitat for Humanity® Peninsula Building Partner

In an effort to support local communities, raise awareness and funds, Morgan James Publishing donates one percent of all book sales for the life of each book to Habitat for Humanity. Get involved today, visit **www.HelpHabitatForHumanity.org.**

DEDICATION

To Justin and Heather who helped me understand and admire the teenage years.

For teens everywhere who are living, loving, laughing, learning, and leading.

Shine on!

Contents

Chapters—*The Gift of...*

PREFACE

This book is for *you!*

A freshman walked up to our Be the Star You Are! charity booth at a high school outreach event and asked if I was Cynthia Brian. When I responded, "Yes", she went on to say how much my first book of this series, *Be the Star You Are! 99 Gifts for Living, Loving, Laughing, and Learning to Make a Difference,* had inspired her. "When are you publishing a book for teens? That would be awesome!" she continued. I regularly receive emails, letters, and calls from teenagers all across America expressing similar sentiments. It was time to take action.

That day I emailed my literary agent and immediately began writing the book. Keeping the same format as the first book, I decided to invite other writers to participate in this venture. After all, I had successfully coauthored the New York Times best seller, *Chicken Soup for the Gardener's Soul,* where we read over 5,000 submissions, editing and rewriting 101 of them. I envisioned a book for teens, about teens, by teens.

How could I help teens be more successful? What were their major concerns? What type of book would they want to read? Since my specialty is coaching youth on acting, writing, presentations, and life skills, I immediately asked clients for feedback. Most of the volunteers of the charity, Be the Star You Are! are teenagers so I had an attentive focus group. Through brainstorming, radio interviews, talking, listening, and reading, this book was born.

Each chapter is by intention very short. You can easily finish it in a few minutes. In every segment you'll find a true story (although some names have been changed) with a simple and fun exercise on how you can implement the lesson into your life, plus a quote to inspire you for the day. You'll discover your passions, conquer your fears, and learn to communicate to accomplish your dreams and goals. Think of me as your guide on the side who believes in you and cheers you to the finish line.

Pick up the book and turn to any page. Be assured that wherever you stop, this is the specific *Gift* you need for today. It's like magic, miracles, and hope all in one package geared specifically for your issues and concerns. There are *free* bonuses just for you at the back of the book, so make sure you check out the web site. With this purchase of ***Be the Star You Are! for TEENS,*** you receive the added feel good advantage of knowing that you are making a difference in the lives of other teens around the planet because the proceeds benefit Be the Star You Are! 501, c3 charity, empowering youth through improved literacy and positive media.

We hope you'll share ***Be the Star You Are! for TEENS*** and heed the wisdom in the Gifts. Give the book as a gift to motivate a friend. Buy copies for your school or library. Organize a book club to discuss the treasures hidden inside. As we like to say, "To be a leader, you must be a reader. Read, lead, succeed!"

Uncover and discover your inner genius with this teen survival guide. I hope you enjoy reading this book as much as I enjoyed writing, compiling, and editing it. We'd all love to hear your thoughts. Thank you for being part of our galaxy. Be the star *YOU* are!

This book is for you. Major in success. Read on!

☆

Visit us at www.bethestaryouare.org or www.bethestaryouare.com.
Write to us at:
Be the Star You Are! 501c3
PO Box 376,
Moraga, California 94556.
Email: Cynthia@bethestaryouare.org

BE THE STAR YOU ARE! LYRICS

Written and composed Kai Esbensen
Performed by Jenny Case

☆

Trust in your heart, believe in your voice.
You make the change when you make the choice.
Dream up your destiny; own the plan.
You know that you will when you know that you can.
Never give up; never give in.
The ones who will work are the ones who will win.
Create the impossible; answer the call.
Go for your everything; give it your all.
Be the star you are, the star you are.
Be the star you are; you are the star.
Make the journey; take the risk; ask for what you need.
Turn setbacks into comebacks; believe and you'll succeed.
Hold up your head; look for the signs.
You'll find all you need in the light that shines.
Believe in yourself in all that you do.
And you'll be the star that's shining for you.
Be the star you are, the star you are.
Be the star you are, you are the star.
Be the star you are, the star you are.
Be the star you are, you are the star.
Keep daring, keep caring.
Keep moving, improving.
Keep giving, keep living.
You are the star.
You are the star.

ACKNOWLEGMENTS

If it takes a village to raise a child, it takes a world to write a book. Writing is a solitary adventure punctuated by the experiences of those we meet in our travels.

Although I toiled alone at my computer for months on end to pen ***Be the Star You Are! for TEENS,*** the book you hold in your hands could not have come to fruition without the generous assistance of many people.

My original acknowledgment section ran over six pages until my noble editor, Eleanor Dugan, advised me to stop gushing my gratefulness. With her counsel in brevity as my directive, I wish to sincerely thank my stellar team: literary agent Bill Gladstone; publisher Morgan James with David Hancock, Jim Howard, Rick Frishman, Robyn Spizman, Sherry Duke, Lyza Poulin, and the design team; editor Eleanor Dugan; photographers Norbert Brein Kozakewycz and Ken Rice; attorneys Greg Axelrud and Marvin H. Kleinberg; Be the Star You Are!® charity board members, advisor Dr. David Loveall, web mistress Kim Carlson, teen chairperson Sujin Park, benefactor Dan Esbensen, and all the volunteers including readers, writers, reviewers, speakers, IT experts, face painters, researchers, radio helpers, social networkers, event strategists, book packers, office assistants, organizers, publicists, donors, and supporters; World Talk Radio production crew, Brandy, Randy, Ruben, Ryan, Jeff, Justin, co-host Heather Brittany, and associate producer, Karalee Webb; *Lamorinda Weekly Newspaper* publishers Andy, Wendy, Lee, and staff; all the talented writers who contributed to this series, and the celebrities who have endorsed my books.

Coming from a big Italian brood was my ultimate fortune. I love and honor my magnificent parents, brothers, sisters, aunts, uncles, cousins, nieces, and nephews. My supreme gratitude goes to my husband, Brian, and children, Justin and Heather, who allow me to be the wild woman I am. Without you, I'd have no stories!

Thanks to all the friends, neighbors, agents, clients, colleagues, benefactors, audiences, radio listeners, guests, teachers, fans, foes, and fellow travelers along this journey of life. As I trot the globe lecturing, I am increasingly convinced that we will find peace on our planet as we all realize that we are living in this world together.

And finally, thank you, readers, especially teenagers, who have made a donation by purchasing this book. You are making a difference for other youth because proceeds from all sales benefit the programs of Be the Star You Are! charity. I hope you are inspired, motivated, informed, and encouraged to reach for the stars and land on them. May you have a grand life knowing that ***you*** are the ***gift.***

Read, lead, and succeed. You are our future. Stay in touch.

BE THE STAR YOU ARE!

In celebration and gratitude,
Cynthia Brian

Executive Director
Be the Star You Are! 501 c3 charity
PO Box 376
Moraga, Ca. 94556
www.bethestaryouare.org
877-944-STAR
Cynthia@bethestaryouare.org

INTRODUCTION

Simple Gifts for Living, Loving, Laughing, Learning, and Leading

You were not created equal. You are something far better. You are unique.

Okay, these are probably not the words you want to hear when you are a teenager attempting to be cool and fit in with the crowd. But before you judge, read on a bit.

The easiest way to mediocrity is to follow the herd mentality. If you want to be happy and successful, you need to stand out from the crowd. And that's what I promise you in ***Be the Star You Are! for TEENS!***—the opportunity to discover your inner greatness. Even if you think you don't excel at anything right now, you'll have a different point of view after reading this book.

Over the years, I have had the privilege of coaching more than 4,500 adolescents, many of them just like you. Each person was different and each one was an individual. Many came to me because they wanted to be an actor or model, others needed help with writing or speaking, and others sought help in overcoming life challenges. All left my office with more self-confidence, self-worth, and self-direction. My dream for you is that, with the help of this book, you'll embrace your individuality while igniting the flame that burns within you, helping you live, laugh, love, learn, and lead a full and happy life of joy and prosperity. Not only is it possible, it is probable.

No one has ever walked this earth with your exact combination of inborn and acquired strengths, weaknesses, skills, foibles, talents, frailties, and experiences. The synergy of all these forces is what makes you strictly one of a kind, an original. And this mixture is the source of your power, providing all the raw materials you need to become a star.

I challenge you to become the star you already are. This book will make you aware of the many gifts you now possess. I won't promise you that living the life you've always dreamed of is easy. In fact, it can be darn hard work. But this book is chock full of the possibilities already within your grasp, offered to you in the form of personal anecdotes, useful tips, and stimulating exercises not only from me, but from many writers just like yourself. Use it as your road map.

It's not easy being a teen in the twenty first century. The media seldom find positive stories to portray about the youth of today. It's up to you to change their focus and their front-page features. Some of the commentary in this book will be unexpected, out of the ordinary, controversial, and definitely different. Hopefully, it will help you think outside the box and reach outside your comfort zone. When you perform the accompanying exercises, please use your imagination, open your heart and mind, and express yourself. Dare to be different. This isn't a test and there are no right and wrong answers. My purpose is to expose you to the innumerable ways you can become your best self, your only true self while discovering and enjoying your star power. I'll provide the guidance. You provide the guts. Together we'll discover the gifts.

I am a storyteller and have always found that by relating true tales of adversity and achievement, triumph and trials, my students remember and comprehend more readily. Throughout the ages, wise storytellers have reawakened the inner spirits of their listeners and inspired them to explore new territories. Stories allow us to dream and give us the courage to act upon our dreams. Stories help us discover and remember meaningful information. A story informs us by simplifying complex issues, ambiguous situations, and opposing forces. Stories often challenge conventional wisdom, showing us people who deviate from traditional practices to produce breakthrough results. Storytelling is as old as humankind, and a strong tradition in my large Italian family.

The stories in this book are all true, although many of the names have been changed to protect the guilty and the innocent. Every contributor adhered to the stringent guidelines of authenticity and factual narrative. These tales of trailblazers offer lessons in living. My hope is that these stories won't end with the telling, but will inspire your own ideas and insights, propelling you to live and retell your own stories based on your unique gifts.

It doesn't matter whether your stories come from growing up in a loving family or from a difficult childhood filled with abandonment and abuse. Today is the first day of *Now* and you are taking a giant step toward creating positive tomorrows. You are enough. You have the *Power* to be the writer, producer, director, and star of your own life. You have the power! Let me write it one more time big and bold... ***You Have the Power!*** You are in charge of your life. You, and only you.

I've anointed you my power partner. The future stars in all my playshops (I don't conduct workshops) must agree to follow three simple rules. Actually I call them tools for living. They are mandatory and I think you'll find them quite entertaining and simple to implement into your jam-packed schedule.

Are you still with me? Great! Here we go.

The Three Tools for Being a Star and Living Your Dream:

1. You must smile.
2. You must have fun.
3. You must be willing to be wild and wacky.

That's it. Those are your new tools. Not hard to follow if you have the grit to stretch, develop, and risk making a fool of yourself. That's exactly what you must do to find your inner fire and live your dream. You are about to meet the more authentic you. You'll be real, listening to your heart and following your inner wisdom to success. How, you may ask, will this system help me be the star that I am or want to be? Simple!

1. Smile

When you smile, you can't be sad. A smile brightens the lives of those you meet, and their joy bounces back to you. A smile helps you see the world in a positive light, which increases your enthusiasm and creativity. A smile exudes confidence and helps you deflect negative interactions. A smile gives your face value.

2. Have Fun

Every moment is more satisfying when you decide to be playful. Having fun is adjusting your attitude so even life's emergencies can be met with style and be seen in perspective. If you choose to be in a good mood and laugh at life, you'll go with the flow and live in the moment more frequently without being flustered or bothered by any curve balls thrown at you...and there will be frequent curve balls.

3. Be Wild and Wacky

This is the most important tool, the one that will make the difference between living Thoreau's "life of quiet desperation" or becoming the star you already are. Being wild and crazy does not mean being "loco en la cabeza". It means taking measured risks and putting yourself in potentially uncomfortable situations that could be beneficial. Go out on that limb to gather the fruit. Ask for what you want, and don't be afraid of failure, remembering that failure is fertilizer. Your biggest crash may lead to your greatest triumph. Learn to laugh at yourself and stretch beyond your wildest imagination. Stop playing it safe, and strive for excellence. Do the unexpected, reaching for the stars and expecting to land on them!

With these three principles you are ready to soar.

Life is our performance. Unfortunately, it offers no dress rehearsals. You're "on stage" all the time—no stopping and starting over. You can improve greatly over time, but you get just one shot at each scene, so you want your performance to be as excellent as possible. You want to be the star of your own production. First impressions are important. The key is passion, preparation, persistence, and practice.

The ultimate goal of ***Be the Star You Are! for TEENS*** is to give you a good kick in the rear to encourage you to live your dreams and never settle for less. You are one of a kind, you are you, you have the power to love yourself and become the person you want to be. You're ready to become the star of your own life when you recognize, use, and enhance your God-given gifts.

"Your Guide on the Side"

I hope you'll find this book a refreshing escape from sermons and rules. Instead, you'll encounter straightforward stories and tools in *simple* easy to read short chapters guaranteed to help you survive and thrive in a rapidly changing, fast paced world. See the universe through others eyes and experience the thrill of living in the moment. Energetic, humorous, informative, and fun, ***Be the Star You Are! for TEENS,*** uncovers and discovers the potential and the genius that *you* possesses.

Open the book anywhere and know that the chapter you find is meant for you today. You'll find simple, short chapters called *Gifts*, each with a practical, playful preparation exercise. Use what works for you and incorporate it into your life. Allow me to be your guide on the side as you navigate the stormy waters of adolescence. It will be smooth sailing.

Go ahead. Take the plunge. The challenge will invigorate you.

Lights! Camera! Action! The spotlight shines on you!

The Gift of
ABILITY

By Cynthia Brian

Since the dawn of civilization, every human who has inhabited this earth has been blessed with distinctive physical and mental abilities. Skills are different from abilities. Abilities are natural born capabilities while skills are learned or taught. A child may have an inborn musical flair, but he or she will become proficient only with training and practice. Unfortunately, in a complex society that equates success with monetary gain, innate aptitudes are often overshadowed by skills that are considered more important for acquiring a high paying job or just earning a living.

The theory that I propose to you is just the opposite. I believe, based on my experience, that when you develop your positive abilities, follow your passions, and do what comes naturally and easily, you will achieve not only a lifetime of happiness, but financial security as well.

J.D. was an average student, preferring to spend his time driving a tractor, mending equipment, helping with the harvest, herding livestock, and going on fire calls with his grandfather, a rancher and volunteer fireman. Known throughout the community for being the "go to" kid when anyone was in trouble, J.D.'s intrinsic strength was solving problems quickly and making others feel safe.

To J.D., lending a hand was no big deal. In one week, he rescued a neighbor's dog who was being attacked by a raccoon, pulled a friend's car out of a muddy ditch, and helped another friend repair a car engine.

J.D.'s teachers didn't consider him college material. He proved them wrong. At college where he was studying agriculture, he was one of only six students chosen to live on and manage the campus farm. At nineteen, he was hired as an engineer at the city fire department, driving the engines and ladder trucks. At the young age of twenty-two, J.D. was recruited by Cal Fire, with a rank of Captain, and a distinctive specialty of heavy equipment operator. His natural abilities for measured risk-taking, ranching, and helping people, combined with his entrepreneurial spirit, and acquired skills of driving and mechanics, were his golden tickets to success. J.D. puts service before self, and is a successful example of constructing a career that emphasizes his discerning qualifications, abilities, and passions.

"When work is a pleasure, life is a joy! When work is a duty, life is slavery." Russian playwright Maxim Gorky said that more than a hundred years ago, and it's truer than ever. Whenever I'm writing, coaching, acting, speaking, or working in the garden, I am so content that I forget what time it is. This tells me that I am using my natural gifts.

What abilities do you possess? What are you doing when you lose track of time? It is your responsibility to discover your numerous talents and use them for the good of yourself and others. Build on your strengths and become an expert in those areas. Every person has unique and special powers. When you add knowledge and put these skills into practice, you'll live a life of meaning *and* you'll making money. Don't let anyone tell you that you don't have what it takes. When you tap into your abilities and believe in yourself and all your possibilities, you can and will achieve your goals.

Not everyone is destined to be a doctor, lawyer, professor, accountant, engineer, business owner, or President of the United States. If we were all clones of one another, not only would the world be a boring place, nothing new would ever be dreamt, discovered, or designed. We need electricians, artists, police, street sweepers, farmers, decorators, cooks, dentists, factory workers, emergency personnel, computer scientists, garbage collectors, landscapers, and actors. The world needs everyone.

Sometimes the hardest person to convince of your abilities is yourself. Ask yourself again what you are good at? What makes your heart skip a beat? Then go out and start living fully. Be outrageous and extraordinary at whatever you do, even if it is flipping burgers. As we often say in the entertainment business, "There are no small parts, only small actors." What's your knack? Implement that special gift.

EXERCISE

A Bargain Way to Build Your Skills

Whatever you are really good at doing, there is a way to practice without paying for an expensive space and instructor. Volunteer! Volunteer at a local charity or non-profit that fits the area you are most interested in. When you help others, you help yourself. Volunteering has the extra benefit of providing you with that "feel good" sensation of actually making a difference. And if you don't like what you are doing, you can always move on to something else. It's like test-driving a car before you buy.

At Be the Star You Are! charity, we want all the volunteers to choose an assignment where they will stretch and thrive. We're not looking for free laborers. We want to grow people. (www.bethestaryouare.org) Check out volunteer opportunities in your city. You may find that you'll receiving extra training free while rehearsing for a career you'll love when your teen years are behind you.

☆

"When you access your abilities
and do what you love,
you'll never work a day in your life!"
Cynthia Brian

The Gift of ACCEPTANCE

By Cynthia Brian

In 1865, with the ending of the Civil War, slavery was abolished in America. In 1920, after three hundred years of being considered second-class citizens, women finally earned the right to vote. In 1968, civil rights leader and orator Martin Luther King, Jr. proclaimed amid race riots "I have a dream!" Forty-one years later, his torch passed to Barack Obama as America inaugurated the first African-American President as the forty-fourth President of the United States. In 2006, it was a proud moment when Nancy Pelosi was elected to the second most powerful post in Washington D.C. as Speaker of the House and in 2009 the Senate voted ninety-four—two to confirm Hillary Rodham Clinton as Secretary of State. The times they are changing!

The movie, *Milk*, nominated for eight Academy Awards, boasts an all-star cast of Sean Penn, Emile Hirsch, Josh Brolin, and James Franco, directed by the veteran director, Gus Van Sant. It was a challenging movie to get made. It deals with gay and lesbian rights and, of course, the first openly gay politician in the United States, Harvey Milk, who was assassinated by a fellow San Francisco Supervisor and former police officer, Dan White. I had the privilege of playing a small part in the film as an Orange County reporter. As I talked with many of the actors and background players on the set, it was obvious that everyone felt this was a movie that needed to be seen. It is time for people to accept and welcome all people regardless of their race, color, religion, beliefs, culture, or sexual orientation.

As I do most years, I was one of the judges for the Emmy Awards. One entry in particular caught my attention. It was a documentary film focused on teens who are gay, lesbian, bisexual, or transgender. The film demonstrated the hatred and discrimination young people face when they admit or are suspected of being part of the non-straight crowd. These kids feared retribution if they "came out" to their families and peers. While understanding and empathy are the building blocks of belonging, family and friends are the foundation. Even when these young people accepted their own sexuality, the outside world did not necessarily accept them. These teens risked losing their friends or being thrown out of their homes if they were inadvertently "outed". What often occurred was these kids were sent to counseling or church where they were asked quirky questions like "Are you sure this is not just a phase?" or were told "Just wait to you fall in love with the right person."

Many religions teach that homosexuality is sinful or against the laws of nature. Is it any surprise that teens feel caught between believing in a loving God and wondering if something is wrong with them?

Susie was a smart beautiful girl who always had the hunkiest boyfriends. In college she married the football star and together they bore four gorgeous children. When the kids were in junior high and high school Susie realized she couldn't live the lie any longer. She told her husband that she was a lesbian and that she had known since age fourteen. Despite her efforts to be straight, she couldn't change her sexual preference. Naturally such an announcement after so many years of marriage was a shock. Had society been more accepting when she was young, this hurtful scenario could have been prevented.

Jorge had a different experience. He was an all-star athlete who had plenty of female dates. From the time he was eight, he knew he was different but didn't know how to express himself. Fortunately for him, he experimented his senior year in high school in a gay relationship. He talked with his family and found acceptance. He went off to college confident in the knowledge that he could be accepted for who he was.

According to the book published by Harvard University Press, *The New Gay Teenager* by Ritch C. Savin-Williams, the average gay adolescent comes out just before or after graduation from high school, although he or she has known for a few years prior. Gay teens have significantly higher rates of both attempts and thoughts of suicide. In his study on gay teen suicide, Patrick Healy concluded that gay teens are "five times more likely to attempt suicide than their heterosexual peers"(2001). As reported in *Lesbian News,* "these youth account for 35 percent of the American population and 15 percent of all suicide deaths"(Ocamb 2001). Of the 4,000 students who were surveyed, 40 percent out of the 10 percent of high school students who attempted suicide were gay. It's a shockingly high number since gay teens comprise just one tenth of the teen population. Because of bullying and name calling, gays and lesbians are more likely to skip school or drop out. Having always to defend one's choices deprives one of personal power. Espousing a non-heterosexual lifestyle does not make a person a deviate or a pervert. The term commonly bantered by teens, "That's so gay!" is hurtful and discriminatory. Mental health professionals have long agreed that rejecting homosexual impulses leads to depression and possible suicide because attempting to alter sexual orientation is unproductive. With life chances limited and intolerance widespread, it is only when we as individuals open our arms and accept everyone exactly the way they are that we can halt this horrendous statistic.

During a class on bigotry, prejudice, and peace, fifteen-year old Joshua raised his hand. Normally shy, he courageously offered his opinion. "Does it really matter if we are Republicans, Democrats, Independents or Green; black, white, yellow, red, or brown; straight, gay, bisexual, asexual; Catholic, Protestant, Muslim, Buddhist, or atheist; dolphin, penguin, elephant, or human? Aren't we all one, living in one world, trying to survive on this planet? If we want to continue to exist we have to learn to accept and embrace our differences. We must stop labeling." At first the class was silent, then applause erupted, followed by an animated discussion.

There is no place for hatred, discrimination, segregation, bigotry, inequality, or prejudice. Intolerance of any kind must not be espoused or endured. To have peace on the planet we must accept our neighbors and treat all people with respect, dignity, and fairness, regardless of their gender, race, color, creed, or sexual orientation.

Tolerance and acceptance start at home. As a nation, we've come a long way, but we have farther to go. If you are a teen needing support, there are many on-campus organizations that cater to your human rights as well as an abundance of useful information on the Internet. Visit http://www.iCelebrateDiversity.com for links to social justice groups promoting equality, anti-racism, anti-poverty, and civil liberties. One comprehensive resource for questions on homosexuality is http://faculty.washington.edu/alvin/gayorg.htm. Here you'll find links to organizations, publications, bookstores, as well as education and health support groups. Another excellent resource is GLSEN, the Gay, Lesbian, and Straight Education Network, http://www.glsen.org. GLSEN is the leading national educational organization focused on ensuring safe schools for all students. Tools, tips, research, a media center, and action steps to protect you from bullying and harassment are just a portion of the assistance they provide.

America has elected a new President of African ancestry. May this be the beginning of a new era of liberty, justice, acceptance, and tolerance for all. Open your eyes and your heart to accept diversity. Practice the Golden Rule and love your neighbor as you love yourself. Put your bias in the trash and walk in someone else's shoes. Accept the dream. This is the true meaning of "Be the STAR you are!

EXERCISE

Accept Yourself, Accept Others

If you find yourself using words or telling jokes that are prejudiced toward another group, stop! Think about how you would feel if someone teased you or disrespected you or your culture. Learn as much as you can about diversity in your area, and welcome people of all beliefs into your circle of friends. Mend a quarrel. Seek out a forgotten soul. Share a treasure. Provide a kind answer. Forgive an enemy. Be kind. Be gentle. Express gratitude. And most of all, accept yourself, accept others, and treat everyone with respect.

☆

"No amount of self-improvement
can make up for a lack of self-acceptance.
When you accept yourself, you'll be able
to accept others unconditionally."
Cynthia Brian

The Gift of
ACHIEVEMENT

By Cynthia Brian

My formal education didn't begin until I was nearly seven, almost four years after most kids. There was no pre-school nor kindergarten near our farm, so first grade was my first exposure to regimented learning. I was an eager student, devouring every tidbit of information and bringing my knowledge home to teach my four siblings and any of the farm worker's children. My fierce determination to learn, combined with a firm work ethic, propelled me to achieve.

My innate abilities were in communicating, organizing, supporting, and leading. Through membership in the 4-H club I learned to sew, cook, decorate, and breed chickens and sheep, while honing my natural aptitudes and leadership skills. When I was sixteen, I was chosen as an exchange student to Mexico where I learned about our neighbors to the south and to converse in Spanish. Speaking another language fluently was high on my list of "to do's". In high school, I was extremely involved in my community and church and in sports and extracurricular activities as well as serving as class Vice President and head cheerleader for three years. By my senior year, I had amassed over 500 various awards and was honored as one of three Outstanding Teenagers of my high school and the Outstanding Catholic Youth in the Diocese of Sacramento. To my utter surprise and extreme delight, I was named The Outstanding Teenager of California, chosen from hundreds of thousands of teenagers in the state. My family and I traveled to the state capitol for the gala ceremony where Governor Ronald Reagan (soon to be the President of the United States) presented me with a heavy trophy that resembled an Oscar. Engraved on the trophy were the words of President John F. Kennedy, "Let the word go forth from this time and place to friend and foe alike, that the torch has passed to a new generation of Americans." Not long afterwards, I was chosen to represent the youth of America as a Teen Ambassador to Europe and "went forth" representing the new American generation in Holland.

Impressing anyone was never my goal. My hunger to improve myself drove my actions. The acclaim was exciting, yet humbling. After all, I was *just* a little farm girl who raised chickens and had a deep desire to realize an education. Those eighteen months in Holland offered me the opportunity to travel throughout Europe, learning foreign languages, culture, history, art, and lifestyles abroad.

When I needed recommendation letters for college admission, I had a brilliant idea. I wrote to my friend, Governor Ronald Reagan asking him if he would consider writing one. He graciously said yes, and I was admitted to the university of my choice, the University of California at Los Angeles, where I studied many things, primarily history and French. In my junior year, I was accepted to the Education Abroad Program. France became my new home for a year. Towards the end of term, again I wrote to the fortieth President of the United States because I hoped to transfer to the University of California at Berkeley to complete my senior year. Once again the great man championed me. It pays to ask for what you want!

Why do I write this brief record of my teen achievements? Because, if I, the chicken lady from a rural area could achieve my ultimate dreams, so can you. Entitlement was not part of my vocabulary. My grandparents had only reached the eighth grade, my parents achieved an education from high school. I was the first in my family to attend college, and I financed the undertaking myself by selling chicken eggs and consistently working. I had nothing handed to me. As an old TV commercial advertised, "I did it the old fashioned way. I earned it." Today I speak several languages and have had the opportunity to travel the world both for business and for pleasure. I am truly living my dreams.

Never accepting "no", hard work, determination, asking for what you want, volunteering to help, honesty, integrity, diligence, and the will to succeed will drive anyone to accomplishment. In fact, all the gifts in this book will help you to achieve your wildest goals if you are willing to put in the time, energy, and effort. If you want advantages in your life, it's up to you to show up and create them.

Are you willing? Only you have the key to your destiny. Others may open doors for you, but only you can walk through them. Are you prepared for success and triumph? Take it from the Chicken Girl …you can do it! You *must* do it! I'm cheering for you!

EXERCISE

The P.E.E.P. Principle

Taking a cue from the chirping of my chickens, I developed *The P.E.E.P. Principle*, a system to help you develop your inborn abilities and a process to acquire the knowledge and skills to power your capabilities towards achievement. P.E.E.P.

stands for passion, energy, enthusiasm, and persistence. Whatever you want to do or accomplish, start by thinking of it in the first-person present tense: "I *am* a designer (or fire fighter or caregiver)." "I *am* a great volunteer (or physical therapist or student)." Talk as if you already are what you want to be. Talking in the future tense—"I'm *going* to be"—is fatal. Before others can believe in you, you must believe in yourself *now*. Be what you want to be by using the first person and the present tense. By the way, there is no *just!*

"You are the writer, producer, director,
and star of your own life.
Conceive, believe, achieve.
You were born to be magnificent!"
Cynthia Brian

The Gift of ADAPTING

By James Christopher Gill

Adjusting to new surroundings can be a trying and painful experience. Because my father's job demanded that we move often, during my youth I was forced to start a new school every couple of years. By the time I reached the seventh grade, I had already attended five different schools. Constantly shifting from place to place was difficult. It seemed like every time I finally settled into a class situation and made new friends, my dad was transferred again. Although it pained my parents to be constantly displacing our family, we uprooted and began the search for a new school in a new town.

I had spent a very happy year in the sixth grade in Los Angeles where I had many good friends and was considered quite popular. In June, my parents announced we were leaving to live in the San Francisco Bay Area. I was devastated as because I knew I had to start all over again to try to adapt to a new world. It took time, but I did adapt.

By ninth grade, other challenges presented themselves. The high school I attended was socially unforgiving. Like many schools, there was a hierarchy pecking order. We called it "the elite, the majority, and the outcasts". I would like to claim that I was somewhere amongst the elite, or even the vast majority, but these would both be lies. Alas, I was considered amongst the outcasts; maybe because I was a bit of a nerd, maybe because I didn't play sports, or maybe because I had long since grown weary of worrying about what other people thought.

In my junior year, we had a new arrival. She was a comely girl from a different state, which immediately elevated her to a person of interest amongst the elite of our school. The boys chased after her, but the girls were envious. Not being naïve enough to fall for the boys' charms and too shy to really embrace her newly found attention, she too, was soon shunned by those whom had most recently embraced her.

I vividly remembered my own challenges coming into a new school, knowing no one, and having no idea how to fit in. Having shared classes with her, I reached out, engaging her in friendly conversation, offering an ear so she could vent her frustrations or simply chat. We developed a friendship those final two years of high school although I never considered myself in her inner circle.

However, one event helped me realize what a profound impact I had had on her tenure at our school.

Our final class together was a creative writing class, and in the closing days of our senior year, our teacher presented an exercise in one individual was given a ball of yarn. The chosen person was instructed to hold on to the end of the string, speak about someone in the class who had positively impressed him or her, then toss the ball of yard to that person. The receiver was to do the same and pass the ball along to someone else until the entire class was bound in a web of good will.

When this young lady's turn came, she held the ball contemplatively for a moment, weighed it in her hands, and looked around the room. She began to speak. She told about arriving at the school and how difficult it was for her to fit in with this new group, having spent most of her formative years in her previous location with her old friends. "It was difficult to start all over and attempt to adapt," she said. Then she looked directly at me and began to speak about the one person who had always made her feel welcome, who had never judged her or expected anything of her, but simply had just been nice to her. "His kindness" she said, "made my transition so much easier." She passed the ball of yarn to me.

In that moment, the pain of all those years of moving about, shifting from school to school, and being the odd man out melted away. My own struggle was worthwhile because I had been able to help one person overcome her angst and adapt.

Life is one long adjustment. Change is challenging, but it usually leads to growth. Being a teenager attempting to acclimate to new surroundings, new schools, and new classmates may be one of the toughest tests, especially if you were comfortable in your last environment and now find yourself unsure of how to fit in. Hang in there. You will survive and you will adapt. And maybe you can help someone else who is having trouble adapting as well.

EXERCISE

The Web of Adaptation

Buy a ball of colorful yarn and gather a group of teens together into a circle. Reach out to people you don't know well and include them in this exercise. The first person holding the yarn says something positive about someone in the group, then tosses the ball of yarn to that person. The person receiving the yarn offers an uplifting comment about someone else and throws the string to the next person. Every person must be a recipient of the yarn. No catty or unkind pseudo compliments allowed, only positive reinforcement. The exercise continues until every person in the sphere is enmeshed in a web of encouraging and constructive remarks. You have designed an adaptive attitude of altitude. You can now spread your wings and fly.

☆

"Growth depends on adaptability.
Be an instrument of adjustment."
James Christopher Gill

The Gift of ADVENTURE

By Billijo Doll

Becoming a Foreign Exchange Student whetted my appetite for adventure.

My families are of German heritage. My grandmothers spoke German to me, and in school I took five years of the language. My mom decided it would be good for me to go to Germany as a foreign exchange student. I thought I could speak German, although I knew I was not fluent.

Let's back up. I was raised as a cowgirl in north central Montana on a cattle ranch. We were eighteen miles from town, six miles from the nearest neighbor, and ten miles to the nearest neighbor with kids. My younger brother and I did not get along, and my younger sister had died. While my brother played upstairs in his attic bedroom, I played outside. My imagination, fueled by the books I read, took me to far away places. My first adventures were in my mind, acted out in my play. They were deep-seated yearnings to explore, to learn, to experience.

I was sixteen when I flew to Germany. I went from Montana to New York City. I saw people of different races I had only seen on television, I heard languages I did not understand, and I heard people speak English with such accents I could not comprehend what they said to me. I saw more people than I had ever seen in my life. I saw skyscrapers for the first time.

I arrived in Frankfort, Germany in a state of bewildered awe. Already I was in culture shock and wowed by all I saw around me! The first question my German family asked me was if I were tired, *"Bist du mude?"* Their German accent was not the dialect I had learned, so I did not understand this very basic question. When we arrived at their home, I was asked if I wanted a *douche* (shower) but I only knew the word with its English meaning and felt even more bewildered and shocked that they would ask me if I needed a feminine hygiene product!

For the next three months, my soul drank in every new venture. I learned their language and experienced a culture that will forever be close to my heart. I saw castles, walled cites, gardens, concentration camps, and cathedrals. I ate new foods that were delicious as well as experimenting with a few dishes that I hope I to never taste again.

I turned seventeen in Germany. I will never forget that garden birthday party with other German teens and the gifts I was given. I still have the teddy bear, and the dirndl (German traditional peasant dress).

What did I learn from my foreign adventure? Most of all, I am grateful that I was born and raised in America where we have freedom of expression and choices in our endeavors. Although Germany was fascinating and beautiful, the population has, because of constant yo-yoing cultural changes, a very strict, disciplined tradition that was strange to me. Despite our differences, I learned to love to explore and to undertake new adventures!

Imagination is the gateway to adventure. As a little girl, I imagined traveling to faraway lands. Because I dreamed it, my imaginings became a reality. A journey to a foreign country helps us grow as individuals while creating a path for understanding, communication, and connection. If we are to have peace in our world, we must stretch with adventures.

I left my home as a cowgirl from rural Montana. After my adventure in Germany, I returned as a *Deutsches Mädchen* (German Girl) with an appetite for diversity. Be bold. Be brave. Travel! Check it out!

EXERCISE

Quest for Adventure

The Gift of Adventure begins in your mind. If you think your life is an adventure—it is. Adventure is a gift of fun, spontaneity, and play. And it is usually more enjoyable when shared with a friend.

Things to try:

★ The next time it is foggy, don a raincoat, grab an umbrella, go for a walk, and pretend you are walking the streets of London. Research on the Internet about England, Jack-the-Ripper, Big Ben, whatever sparks your interest. Sip a cup of tea, nibble a biscuit (shortbread cookie), and speak in an "English accent." Any time the weather is odd for your area, pretend you are somewhere where that weather is normal. Snow storm day, pretend you are in Alaska and try to snowshoe with old tennis rackets tied to your boots. Be creative.

★ On a hot dry day, have a beach party and play volleyball with a beach ball. There are no limits to adventures of the imagination.

★ Attend cultural events in your city—learn about foreign cultures, decide what foreign country you want to visit, and start preparing to go there, even if there seems no possible way you would get the chance to go.

★ Try new things. If you like rap music, risk attending an opera performance.

★ Take classes to learn a new language or at least the important words—"where is . . . restaurant/hotel/toilet/station/shower . . ."

★ Reach out in friendship to at least three people outside your close circle.

Go on an adventure while staying at home. Discover the thrill of exploration.

☆

"Go! Learn! Explore!
Imagination is the
gateway to adventure."
Billijo Doll

The Gift of AFFIRMATION

By Davis Lunsford

As a child, which was only a few years ago, I always looked forward to any time my name or picture was printed in our small town newspaper, *The Graham Leader,* not just for a tiny bit of fame and recognition. I had another reason. Every time my name appeared in the newspaper, a letter appeared in my mailbox. The letter would be from Pastor Joe Finfrock. With delight, I'd tear into the letter and look over its contents: a copy of the newspaper clipping (with my name highlighted) a handwritten letter, and a dollar bill. Pastor Joe invariably offered congratulations and encouragement for my achievement, be it winning a baseball game, doing a Cub Scout service project, or participating in the library's book club. At the bottom of the note, beneath the dollar bill, he always scribbled, "Here, buy a Coke on me."

I know Pastor Joe has touched hundreds of other children through the same type of letter. I would expect that he is one of the leading supporters of the town's postal, soda, and dental industries. Sometimes, the letters would even contain two or three dollars and the note, "Here, buy you and your friends a Coke on me."

Pastor Joe doesn't limit his affirmations, as these emotional boosts are now called, to people who appear in the newspaper. Graduations, birthdays, marriages— in Pastor Joe's book, they're all occasions for a note. When I earned my Eagle Scout rank from the Boy Scouts of America, I received a letter from Pastor Joe congratulating and encouraging me to keep living by the values that had brought me this far.

I think affirmation is one of the gifts people enjoy most. Yet few people are consistently affirmative. Everyone has received phone calls, letters, or text messages that offer praise. They make you feel special. They let you know others are thinking of you. They reinforce your resolve to stand for your beliefs. Affirmation can turn a bad day or a bad attitude completely around.

We could all learn from Pastor Joe. Affirmation is a powerful gift and so inexpensive to give. It doesn't require a dollar bill to be effective. Just acknowledge positive things people are doing. Affirmation can inspire others and even yourself. You can support others through actions, attitudes, spoken words, letters, emails, and gifts. Affirming yourself can keep you moving when circumstances get tough.

Pastor Joe doesn't have any more minutes in his day than other people, yet he takes the time to bless others. Pastor Joe has the habit of affirming, and the habit of affirming is the habit of affecting and inspiring lives. You may never know how much hearing an encouraging word can bless someone. Take the time to affirm people, and both you and they will be rewarded.

EXERCISE

Cheerleading 101

Get out your stationary and write three letters:

★ Write the first letter to someone who has encouraged you in the past. Thank them for their gift. Affirm their affirmation.

★ Write the second letter to anyone—anyone who you would like to affirm. You can write to someone who has just accomplished something, or someone who you think needs encouragement. Affirm by cheering for something positive they've done. Consider including a dollar bill in your letter as an added bonus.

★ Write the third letter to yourself. Pick something positive you've been doing.

Congratulate yourself for your good work, and encourage yourself to continue.

☆

"Affirmation is the sunlight of the soul,
without which we cannot bloom or grow."
Davis Lunsford

The Gift of AMUSEMENT

By Cynthia Brian

Golf is *not* my sport. I always felt that golf was something you took up when you were old and couldn't run anymore. Besides, I have no patience or desire to spend my time chasing little white balls. Oh yes, I've heard all the public relations about how great it is to be out in nature, talking to friends, and making business deals. But it wasn't until I heard teenage friends singing the praises of golf that I paid attention.

Tiger Woods has made the game of golf interesting and accessible to adolescents and the junior golf game is a growing trend. More young people than ever before are taking up the sport. In fact, many teens are applying for and receiving scholarships to major universities because of their prowess on the greens.

At a school fund raising auction, I decided to bid on a week's vacation to Fairmont Hot Springs in the Canadian Rockies, in a remote area of eastern British Colombia. The Rocky Mountains loom large on one side. The Columbia River is resplendent on the other—a very picturesque and restful place...with *golf* as its main attraction.

After we had exhausted the hiking trails, the mineral springs, and the tennis courts, the teens in the group thought we should try a few rounds of golf. "No," I protested, "I *hate* golf. It's for old fogies, and I'd rather read a book."

"Oh, come on," they begged. "You'll be great. You're a natural athlete, and its better to learn a game when you're young. " Glad they thought I was still young. So off we went to play my first round of golf.

The setting was majestic, very wooded, and green. Being the gardener I am, I found myself pulling up any weeds I saw. The first few holes went really well. I beat par. "See, we told you you'd get the hang of it," my amused partners purred.

"You know," I boasted, "I always was a champion miniature golfer as a kid. I was unbeatable." They looked at one another and together gave me a funny look. We continued playing, and I admit I was kind of enjoying it by the time we arrived at the ninth hole next to a lake. The object of this hole, I was told, was to hit the ball across the lake and land on the fairway on the other side. Each person took a swing, landing the ball perfectly. Now it was my turn.

Being an aggressive softball player, I stood over the ball, took aim, and whacked it like I was driving for a home run. What happened next could probably never be duplicated without special effects. The ball flew across the lake, ricocheted off a tree into a wooden bridge, rebounded into another tree, and arched gracefully back over the lake, landing squarely at my feet. All this happened in a few seconds while we stood trying to follow the ball's path. It was like a cartoon.

We looked at one another and began to laugh. We laughed so hard that we collapsed on the course. Other golfers joined in until the ground was littered with convulsing bodies gasping for breath between roars of laughter. "Do it again!" the kids chanted. Fat chance! It was obvious that my golf career was over. For that matter, I think it is safer for the rest of the world if I stick to miniature golf, softball, or gardening. Unless you want a day of hilarious amusement, then I'm the perfect golf partner.

Make time for mirth every day. Humor is food for the soul. Numerous medical studies indicate that the deep breaths we take and the chemicals our body releases when we giggle hasten healing and reinforce the body's immunity. When you are having a bad day, rent several funny DVD's, and chuckle your way to amusement. You'll feel so much better once you've released those happy endorphins. As teens, we often take ourselves too seriously, worrying too much about school, getting into college, peer pressure, clothes, dating, and being cool. Forget it about it. Decide to have a good time, eliminate the boredom, amuse yourself with glee, and you'll find your troubles melt away.

Opportunities for amusement are everywhere, in everything, everyday. Hilarity is a healing drug with no side effects. Take a swing at unabashed laughter—it's free!

EXERCISE

Amusement Muse

For this exercise, grab your stomach and laugh, laugh, laugh until your laughter is real and unforced. Your cares will melt away. An alternate game requires a partner. Look at each other and play, "Whatever you do, don't smile!" No matter how hard you try, you'll both soon be giggling helplessly. When you can stop, wipe the tears from your eyes and go forth, refreshed and stress free. Amusement and merriment are food for the soul.

☆

"You don't stop laughing because you grow old.
You grow old because you stop laughing."
Cynthia Brian

The Gift of APPRECIATION

By Neha Patel

Dear Cynthia Brian,

My name is Neha Patel, and I am truly interested in helping your organization. My mother bought and read your book titled ***Be The Star You Are! 99 Gifts for Living, Loving, Laughing, and Learning to Make a Difference.*** She absolutely loved it!

It has been an inspiration to my whole family to keep on growing and dreaming. Throughout my teen years my mom would read me stories from your book. The stories helped to lift my mood when I would just feel like giving up or quitting. You see, I suffer from depression, schizophrenia, and OCD (obsessive/compulsive disorder), and after I was diagnosed four years ago, my family lost their strength and vigor to keep on fighting. It seemed that our entire world had fallen apart.

My mother, father, and sister were so saddened that I had to start living with a chronic illness at the young age of sixteen. They almost gave up hope. Thankfully, my mom came across some truly inspiring stories, one of them being your book, and she not only started fighting, but helped me fight as well.

Everyone in my family gained courage from the words in your book. We started looking at life's struggles as blessings in disguise. My mom and I would sit down together and laugh at the funny experiences in your book. Every day, we made it a habit to just open the book at any particular spot, and read the story that we came across. Your stories would help comfort me when I was feeling down, and helped encourage me to achieve greater heights. Living with a mental illness, I have to listen more to my heart than my head. Having said this, I know I want to help others achieve success, too.

Right now, I am in my third year at community college where I am studying mathematics and psychology. I honestly believe your book has helped bring out the best in my family and me. The reason I am telling you all this is because your book has played a major role in my decisions. When a week seems unbearable, I think about the words in your book, and feel encouraged. ***Be The Star You Are!*** taught me to follow my dreams. It helped me realize that every day is a learning experience. I believe that with your book as my guide, I will be able to make better decisions.

I consider it an honor to have the opportunity to write to you, and I deeply want to thank you for all your encouraging words of wisdom and support. My debt to you will probably never be repaid, but just knowing that there is a way to give back to others keeps me going. Is there any volunteer job that I might be able to help you and your organization with? It would be a privilege to work with you and Be the Star You Are! charity. Thank you so much for your kindness and encouragement. I am truly blessed to have come across an individual of your caliber.

Sincerely,
Neha Patel

EXERCISE

Appreciation Station

Have you ever read a book, watched a movie, or heard a song that really changed your life? Take a moment to show your appreciation by writing a letter or sending an email to the author, actor, or musician who inspired you. Do a search on the web to find out where to send your note. You may receive a response but even if you don't, you have expressed yourself. Whatever challenges you face in life, there is help available. You'll find inspiration in books, music, lectures, movies, and individuals when you are willing to seek uplifting, spirit enhancing messages and positive role models. Seek medical attention and professional counseling if you are depressed or sick. Give back to others by volunteering for a charity that you believe in. Be positive and affirming because you never know how you might be stimulating greatness in another person. Life is what you make it and there is nobody just like you. You will bring pleasure to the lives of others when you show your appreciation. And it's possible, that just like my letter to Cynthia that you are reading in this book, your greetings of appreciation will be published. What a beautiful surprise and gift back to me this is!

☆

"To the world you might be one person,
but to one person you just might be the world.
Appreciate everyone and everything."
Cynthia Brian

The Gift of ATTITUDE

By Kim Carlson

My dad grew up a scrappy kid with an attitude, but he was also just about the funniest person I ever knew. He was a true word gymnast, constantly on the lookout for a comical way to turn a phrase. Instead of scolding the five of us kids for not finishing our vegetables, he'd say, "eat every carrot and pea on your plate!" (Think about it.) As soon as we caught the double meaning, we'd start giggling, and soon our dinners disappeared.

My mom, on the other hand, was raised on a farm in the Midwest and grew up to be a very introspective, intelligent, and reserved person. She wanted to be a doctor...or a goatherd. In any crisis, you could always count on her to be calm and collected. Hers was a very different attitude, and I learned a lot from both my parents.

When Dad was eight years old, he was cornered in an alley by three thirteen-year-olds wanting a fight, but Dad came out the winner. It was his scrappy attitude that allowed him to prevail.

When I was eight years old, I had my own ordeal to overcome. It was moving day, and my sisters and I went next door to say goodbye. I reached down to give a pat on the head to their little terrier, and she jumped at my face. I felt her bump into my cheek, and then I put my hands to my face and came away with blood all over them. I was scared, but Mom was very calm, as usual, even though I bled all over the brand new carpet. She got me cleaned up, showed me the wound in the mirror, noticed that I had lost a tooth as well, and took me to the doctor for stitches. That night, we put a note under my pillow explaining that the dog had eaten my tooth. The tooth fairy was very nice to me.

By her example, Mom showed me how to be calm, cool, and collected during a crisis. But Dad advised me, "If a dog ever tries to bite you again, bite it back!" I learned to be tough from my dad, to fight off adversity, and to do it all with a sense of humor. The scrappy attitude and the calm attitude blended wonderfully in me, like oil and vinegar. The day of the dog bite, combined with a sense of humor and a vinaigrette attitude, helped me develop some super powers.

When I was twelve years old, I needed prescription glasses. At first I was horrified and embarrassed. I avoided being seen in my glasses for a long time. But the moment I remembered to bite that "dog" back, and stop allowing fear to take over was when I decided that, instead of poor eyesight, I had *Microscope Vision*, my first super power! I can see near objects better than anyone I know. I can take a sliver out of your hand without a magnifying glass, and I can see every whorl in a fingerprint. Amazing! As soon as I had developed that super power, no one even seemed to notice I was wearing glasses.

I got braces when I was fourteen, and I had another opportunity to overcome embarrassment with attitude. Instead of trying to hide my smile, I just acted like nothing had changed, and for about the first three days, not even my best friends noticed I had all that metal in my mouth. This super power is a *Cloaking Device*!

Just like my dad, I enjoy giving a humorous twist to life, and every time I have a hurdle to overcome, I develop a new super power. Not only is it helpful to have a good attitude when you're facing a problem, a positive attitude can be fun and funny, healthy and healing. You can feel strong and powerful if you try being scrappy like my dad while staying calm like my mom.

For Spiderman, it all started with an accidental bite from a radioactive spider. I got my super powers after being bit by a little dog and getting an infusion of oil and vinegar attitudes. Put a little salad dressing on your attitude, throw in a good dose of humor, and you, too, can become a super hero!

EXERCISE

I Am Powerful

I know a lot about adversity. I have Fibromyalgia and a lot of food intolerances, and therefore a lot of restrictions about what I can do and what I can eat. But I choose to ***not*** see them as restrictions. Rather, I see them as opportunities for creativity and invention, and I make some amazing gourmet meals out of simple ingredients. A positive attitude and a healthy diet go a long way toward overcoming my aches and pains.

It's time to get your dander up and fight *your* adversity.

First, name the "dog that bit you." Yours might be a physical challenge like mine, or maybe there's a classmate who makes you feel bad, a family member who teases you, or any number of situations that might be taking your positive energy away.

Now picture yourself as an animal. It's your choice, but it should be a powerful animal like an elephant, whale, lion, wolf, or grizzly bear. Be creative and choose a kindred beast. At the same time, keep your cool, stay calm, and develop your power. Stay stealthy and breathe in the energy.

Think about this as you breathe: a person or situation cannot force you to feel bad. You feel bad because you are giving away your power to the person or situation. You don't need to let someone or something control how you feel. Take back the power you have given away. Say the following as many times as it takes:

You have no power over me! *You Have No Power Over Me*! ***You Have No Power Over Me!***

And finally, remember your sense of humor and eat every carrot and pea on your plate.

☆

"Adjust your attitude and claim your power!"
Kim Carlson

The Gift of BEAUTY

By Cynthia Brian

You've heard it said that "beauty is only skin deep" and "beauty is in the eye of the beholder". Even though we all tend to judge a book by its cover to some degree, what is actually important is what's written in the pages. Everyday we are bombarded by the media with images of what the current beauty status quo is.

I don't know about you, but beauty magazines make me feel ugly. Every magazine from *Cosmo* to *Seventeen* to *Vogue* offers beauty tips on how to make us more irresistible to the opposite sex.

No matter how much I weigh, what makeup I wear, or what clothes I buy, I never look as gorgeous as the models portrayed. And yet…I *am* one of those models! For years, I have worked modeling, acting, appearing in print and commercials. I have a secret to share with all of you—all of us are incredibly imperfect. Over the years I've worked with the beautiful women and men who are held in high esteem for their fashion and good looks. They too have cellulite, pimples, bags under their eyes, and life problems. Ironically, many suffer from poor body image, anorexia, and bulimia in their quest to book the job and appear beautiful. What's worse, these images of ultra thin, gaunt men and women have ignited a scourge of devastating eating disorders and feelings of worthlessness throughout much of the world. It may be no irony that in the English language the word *die* is part of the word *diet.*

One time I was hired for a fancy jewelry ad where close ups of my neck and face were required. Right before the shoot, a mosquito bit me on my cheek leaving a huge, ugly bump that couldn't be hidden with makeup. "No problem," said the photographer, "we'll airbrush you!" Sure enough, when magazines published the full-page advertisement, my face looked absolutely perfect. Not a single enlarged pore, no hair out of place, perfectly lined full lips, and extra deep blue eyes stared back at me. A stunning beauty to all who witnessed the photography, but I knew better.

Once on a movie set with high profile actors, a young unattractive ingénue arrived and sat down in the principle movie star's chair. "Excuse me", I whispered to the lost girl, "extras are gathering in the ballroom. This green room is for the leads." She looked at me and whispered back, " I am…!" She *was* the star of the film. How embarrassing, but without her fancy makeup and hair, she was totally unrecognizable.

Once she emerged from the makeup trailer, she looked like the exquisite beauty we see on screen, on TV, and in the magazines. We bonded over that moment as I applauded her willingness to be real off the set. She responded by saying "being a celebrity 24/7 is not all that it is cracked up to be."

Some friends had a lovely standard poodle diagnosed with osteo sarcoma. The veterinarian advised amputating its leg, but the parents of the family felt it would be better to euthanize this beloved pet. The children were outraged. "She's part of the family, we can't put her to sleep!" they implored. The mother responded, "But she won't be pretty anymore." The youngest daughter retorted, "Of course she'll be pretty. Nothing will change on the inside, and she'll always be beautiful and special to us." The kids won, and the parents learned a valuable lesson.

What I have discovered, is that beauty is an inside job, and you can be awesome at any age, whether you are thirteen or thirty, fifteen or fifty, eighteen or eighty. When you have a positive outlook, adopt an attitude of gratitude, enjoy close relationships, tap into your spirituality, manage stress, exercise sufficiently, and eat nutritionally balanced meals, your body, mind, and spirit will glow.

Makeover shows on television are prolific. You don't need a magazine, movie, or television program to bring out your attractiveness. Being beautiful is not about plastic surgery, your makeup, hair, and clothing styles. It's about taking care of you, loving the person inside, being healthy, and serving others. Take a look in the mirror and admire yourself. You are a wonder of creation

Before she died, I had the privilege to work on a movie and interact with the legendary Belgian born, Dutch and British raised actress, Audrey Hepburn, who starred in such renowned films as *Breakfast at Tiffany's*, *Wait Until Dark*, and *My Fair Lady*. Ranked as the third greatest female star of all time by the American Film Institute, Ms. Hepburn is one of only a few performers to have won an Oscar, Grammy, Emmy, and Tony as well as posthumous awards for her humanitarian work. Her beauty tips are indelibly embedded in my heart and make a flawless beauty ritual for you.

For attractive lips, speak words of kindness.

For lovely eyes, seek out the good in people.

For a slim figure, share your food with the hungry.

For beautiful hair, let a child run his/her fingers through it once a day.

For poise, walk with the knowledge that you never walk alone.

People, even more than things, have to be restored, renewed, revived, reclaimed, and redeemed;

Never throw out anyone.

Remember, if you ever need a helping hand, you will find one at the end of each of your arms.

As you grow older, you will discover that you have two hands; one for helping yourself, and the other for helping others.

Be the most beautiful you!

EXERCISE

Beauty Basics

Age is something that doesn't matter unless you are cheese. Adopt these simple strategies of a makeover magic to extol your beauty from the inside out and you'll be beautiful forever. Beauty basics include:

★ Positive Attitude
★ Social Support System
★ Spirituality
★ Exercise
★ Nutrition
★ Stress Management
★ No Smoking Please
★ Drink Lots of Water
★ No Drugs
★ Be Sun-Smart
★ Sleep Tight
★ Volunteer
★ Floss and Smile
★ Have Regular Check-ups

- Pet a Pet
- Read Empowering Books
- Go Easy on Makeup

Pamper yourself. Discover the fountain of youth and beauty. Your body is a tabernacle. Protect and honor it. Be awesome at any age!

☆

"Take a look in the mirror
and admire yourself.
You are a wonder of creation.
Beauty is an inside job!"
Cynthia Brian

The Gift of BREATHING

By Justin Murray

"Ooh, there must be an accident on 285, take a look." Slowly, regally, the boy turns his head to face where his father is pointing. His feet are flat and firm against the floor of the car, his jaw is tight, and the tilt of his head makes him observe his nose rather more than the scene before him.

Yes, there can be no doubt: in cold fury, I look completely ridiculous. Why am I angry? God alone knows. Something about not reading enough, no one cares. I am angry, and my preposterous countenance displays it.

I take deep breaths and gradually begin to calm down, de-prioritizing my nose and beginning to watch the cars fly past. With a few more breaths, I begin to think. Before I know it, I'm not angry anymore.

It's funny, isn't it, how breathing can calm you? One would think that if calming were as simple as breathing, nobody would ever get worked up (since I don't know anybody who stops breathing for a long period without side effects).

Back in the car, I frown. Why, I ask myself, can breathing calm you sometimes? I chew my lower lip, pondering. I suppose it's like a baby being rocked; we probably just like the rhythm. No, that can't be it. I've seen angry people listen to rap, which is all rhythm, and they practically go into a frenzy. Maybe it's biological? That would make sense. As we breathe, we replenish the oxygen supply in our brains, so we think more clearly and lose our anger in reason.

Who am I kidding? Do I feel an iota more reasonable now than I did when I was angry? Well, maybe, but that's not the point. Angry people breathe deeply, too, and some anger is justified. You can't drown righteous anger in reason, but breathing quiets all anger. What, then, is the key?

A memory comes to my mind. I see myself in the dojang (martial arts training room), down on my knees on the mat with the rest of the school. We are peace breathing. The technique involves kneeling on a mat, breathing in and out, and waving our arms in a moderately silly manner, like a breaststroke pull. Peace breathing is obviously intended to induce a peaceful feeling, and it works. Why?

I make the connection. Why does kneeling, breathing, and waving your arms around calm you? What healing powers are in walking, humming, playing the piano, or any of the other things people do to calm themselves? Why do I feel calm now, tapping away on a BlackBerry, recording my thoughts as they come to me?

Because, I'm good at it. People are calmed by what they can do. A pianist is soothed by a piano, a writer finds solace with a pen or a thumb keyboard, and walking comforts a hiker. Peace breathing works because we do what we're good at, and everybody can be good at kneeling, breathing, and waving their arms around. Everybody's good at breathing, and that's what makes it such a great gift.

It sounds odd, but breathing anchors our world. When we're in emotional turmoil, we breathe deeply, conscientiously, and suddenly we're back on familiar turf. Breathing is a miracle. While fulfilling a life function, it provides us with a perfect opportunity to give any situation familiarity, and thereby comfort. The worst road is the road untrod, the unknown path. But sitting here, BlackBerry in hand, I see that we can release any stress, traverse any hardship, if we just realize that, whatever is different, we've been on other roads before, and we're still breathing.

EXERCISE

Peace Breathing

To soothe your soul and relax your body, incorporate peace breathing into your daily routine.

- Kneel. The tops of your feet should be flat on the floor. Put your knees and ankles together with your legs fully folded beneath you so that your torso is over your lower calves.
- Close your eyes. Bring your hands up in front of you.
- Push slowly to the sides with your arms. As you do so, exhale slowly through your mouth. Make a small but prolonged gasping sound as you do, so that you can hear yourself breathing.
- When your arms are fully extended, bring them slowly in front of you. Keep exhaling. By the time your hands meet, your lungs should be empty.
- Now bring your hands slowly to your face, breathing in through your nose. Your lungs should be full when your hands reach your chest. You may now begin again, pushing to the sides and exhaling.
- Repeat the breathing procedure until you feel calm and peaceful.

☆

"Everybody's good at breathing. Breathe deeply!"
Justin Murray

The Gift of CHALLENGES

By Shirley Cheng

Can mountains really block you, or can you transform them into valleys of gold? After scaling heaven knows how many slopes, hills, and mountain ranges, I can personally assure you that not only can you triumphantly savor your conquests atop the highest peak, but crown yourself as an emperor of endless golden valleys. How could I be so certain? Well, I scaled my mountains, all the while being blind and wheelchair-bound.

I encountered my first mountain when I contracted severe juvenile rheumatoid arthritis at only eleven months old, leading me to a mountain range I constantly climb even to this date: from initial knife-cutting pain and near death in my early years to daily inconveniences and discomforts now.

Once I had prevailed over my physical pain through the unconditional love and unwavering support of my mother, Juliet Cheng, more challenges barged into my life.

After years of hospitalization, I started schooling for the very first time at age eleven when my health was finally stabilized. Back then, I knew only my ABCs and very simple English; I knew that two plus two equaled four and that three times five was fifteen; I had no idea from where rain came from and why a beautiful rainbow soon followed.

Wanting to learn as much as I could as quickly as possible, I absorbed all that was taught in class and mostly self-taught myself how to read. My thirst for knowledge paid off in about 180 days of attendance in elementary school when I mastered grade level and eagerly entered middle school with a smile that spoke a thousand words.

As if the mountains I climbed were not enough to test my spirit, life veiled my eyesight at age seventeen. Instead of letting this challenge hinder me from going for my gold medals, I simply opened another door. It led me to rewards and awards of every kind.

During the deterioration of my eyesight, I learned by listening to my teachers as they taught math, chemistry, and French. When my eyesight completely forsook me in tenth grade, I had no choice but to stop attending school and receive home tutoring. I completed all my assignments using cassettes and recorders. I also successfully wrote and calculated long chemistry equations in my head without Braille.

To my dismay, even though I earned an overall average of 97% or 3.9 GPA, I couldn't accumulate enough credits to graduate, so I pursued a high school equivalency diploma instead. I took the entire GED exam, including mathematical calculations and problem solving, graphs, and an essay, without vision or Braille. My exceptional 3280 on the test earned me a special recognition award.

When life took away my eyesight, I was determined to give birth to a new vision. Now, at age twenty-five, I'm an author and contributor to twenty-four books and winner of fourteen awards. I use a screen reader (computer software) and my two index fingers to produce sixty-five words per minute. I've also completed every step of book production, from formatting my manuscripts to designing and maintaining my own website.

Now, looking down from the top of the world on my accomplishments the from the top of the world, I conclude that challenges are life's vaccines: they exercise your spirit to help you withstand high winds and equip your soul with the necessary tools to battle future storms. I've received many of these vaccines; the obstacles have left numerous scars on my body in all shapes and sizes, but these marks have made me stronger and more invincible as I search for the next high mountain to scale.

If there were no challenges, how could I name myself a champion? If there were no darkness, how could the stars appear so bright?

EXERCISE

Climb Any Mountain

Whenever you meet a new mountain, take the following steps to scale it:

★ Calm down to focus on what you want to achieve. Focus your energy on how to improve your situation.

★ Fight challenges with positivity. Think about something that you're grateful for, that makes you happy, that you love, and then replace any negative thought with the positive one.

Keep these points in mind as you face your obstacles:

- ★ There's always someone out there who's in a much worse situation than you, so be thankful for your own situation, for what you have and the people who are around you.
- ★ You're not enduring alone. Millions of people are battling challenges this very minute, from the homeless on the streets to the sick in hospitals. And there may be people going through the same difficulty you're experiencing now.
- ★ Everything passes, and so will your current negative situation. Why waste your energy on something that will be gone tomorrow?

Above all else, have deep, unwavering faith in God Almighty; it's the ultimate secret to success. It's faith in God that will allow you to move forward, one sure step at a time. When you keep your faith in God strong and steady, no mountain will be high enough to hold you back and no wind will be strong enough to blow you down.

☆

"Although I'm blind, I can see far and wide;
even though I'm disabled,
I can climb high mountains.
Let the ropes of hope haul you high!"
Shirley Cheng

The Gift of CHOICE

By James Christopher Gill

On February 6, 2003, I endured one of the post painful experiences of my entire life. A little after 11 PM, a drunk driver, with a blood alcohol content approximately twice the legal limit, smashed into my vehicle in a head on collision. She crossed over two lanes of traffic and the middle turn lane to meet my car in a horrific crash.

The effect was instantaneous. My right ankle was shattered, two bones turned literally into dust. My foot was dislocated, and my kneecap was broken into two pieces. I was immobilized, in a state of shock.

I tried to get out of my car, but found that my right leg was unresponsive. I pulled it out from under the damaged dash and set myself to walk out of the car. I immediately crumpled to the ground in agony. Fortunately, good Samaritans stopped and assisted me to the side of the road. The police soon arrived, and eventually the paramedics.

At the hospital where, I had to wait for eight hours before proper pain medication was administered. Surgery followed for open wounds on my knees. Insisting that they needed to wait until the swelling had subsided on my ankle, the medical team didn't diagnose my dislocated foot for four days. Then through a blur of immense pain, I heard them say that my foot might amputation.

After being discharged from the first hospital, I was relocated to a facility nearer home. Four more surgeries. Three were on my ankle and metal pins were placed into my foot. Five more months of agonizing pain followed.

I did my best to remain strong. Throughout this time of suffering, the support of my friends and family helped me find the strength within myself to stay positive.

When the doctors told me they had to cut off my foot, I told them emphatically "No! I would rather have half a foot than none at all." When they told me that I would never run or jog again, I told them to try and stop me. Throughout my life I've always been active. I've played competitive sports as well as training for ten years to achieve my black belt in Shoalin Kempo. My choice to remain whole never wavered.

I refused to accept limitations. I dedicated myself to my physical rehabilitation. I stayed positive with my friends and family. I made those choices.

Today, only seven years later, I am as strong and healthy as before the accident. I believe that my positive outlook and personal desire was the one thing that has allowed me to continue to live the life I've always wanted.

Author Denis Waitley said, " There are two primary choices in life: to accept conditions as they exist, or accept the responsibility for changing them." Either you chose to be a victim, or you chose to be proactive. You never know what hurdles you may have to jump. What you do with your circumstances is up to you. It is not what happens to you that determines your destiny. It is your response that makes the difference. We always have choices and choices shape who we become.

The choices we make are our sole responsibility. I chose to believe that the only thing that could ever stop me was myself. And I was right!

EXERCISE

Pro Choice

Think of a situation that requires you to make a choice. On a piece of paper draw three columns and label them as follows:

- ★ Circumstance
- ★ What others recommend
- ★ What I want

Document your answers honestly. Review your choices, and then make an informed decision. Be proactive and make a beneficial choice.

☆

"Choice is power. Choose wisely."
Cynthia Brian

The Gift of COMMUNICATION

By Cynthia Brian

Over lunch one day, a prominent author friend of mine told me how he became a writer. As a child, he was rather scrawny and not very athletic. Other kids teased him, calling him a sissy. His father was ashamed of raising a son who was considered a wimp.

One day he announced, "Richard, I'm sending you away to military school to make a man out of you!" The son begged and pleaded with his folks to no avail. They were determined to make a macho man of Richard. In desperation, just days before he was to be shipped off to the military academy, Richard tried a last ditch attempt. He sat down and wrote an impassioned, detailed letter to his parents succinctly explaining exactly why military school would destroy him in body, mind, and soul. He implored his parents to allow him to follow a path of his own choosing. His parents read the letter. Then they reread it. They were so moved by Richard's words that they cancelled his appointment with the academy and Richard realized his potential as a writer. Richard had learned the power of communication.

You know Richard as Richard Nelson Bolles, the "internationally acclaimed" best selling author of *What Color is Your Parachute?* Dubbed the Business Bible, (www.jobhuntersbible.com) his book has graced best-seller lists for four decades, has been translated into ten languages, and has sold millions of copies. He is a master communicator, traveling the world lecturing and inspiring audiences to find their passion. It all started with that one letter to his parents. And, by the way, Richard grew to be a hunk of man at six feet, five inches!

4-H clubs sponsor annual demonstrations where members are judged on their ability to convey useful information with conviction on their chosen subject. I was only nine when I entered my first competition, chattering about my chickens. It took me weeks to design and perfect my presentation, and more weeks to create the storyboards. I was nervous at the idea of addressing several judges plus an auditorium of seasoned professionals.

That year I won first place and went on to win county, regional, and state competitions. Boosted by the confidence that winning anything provides and also knowing that any monetary honorarium would help me towards my goal of attending college, I practiced my communications skills by entering writing, speaking, and performance competitions. The Lion's Club, Rotary, Knights of

Columbus, Kiwanis, and other service groups sponsored yearly contests, and I applied for them all. Some I won, some I lost, but I always learned more about myself. Every opportunity perfected the craft of communication.

Learning to communicate effectively is essential for every aspect of personal and business associations. Communication involves active listening as well as understanding. To be heard, you must listen. When you listen, others learn to talk. The sooner you understand that everyone communicates not only with words, but also with body language, tonality, and spirit, the more successful you will be in your encounters with others.

Do your parents get on your nerves when you try to talk with them? Has your best friend told one of your sacred secrets to your most ferocious rival? Are you feeling like you are on a cultural collision course when speaking to your teachers? Why can't you say what you mean to say? Like so many of us, you probably have not learned to communicate effectively. For young people, communication has become all about technology—texting, instant messaging, emails, and the Internet which may hinder valuable interpersonal communiqué.

Statistics from the November 2008 eMarketer report indicated that by 2012, 22.2 million teens will use the Internet, up from 20.2 million in 2008. Those under age 13 will have represent 127.4 million users as opposed to 15.6 million in 2008. Youth represent almost 20 percent of total Internet consumers in the United States. How are young people communicating? While 78 percent plus of adults thirty-five or older use email, 42 percent of young people use text messaging as their preferred communication.

My specialty has been coaching young people to express themselves skillfully and with passion by teaching them specific methods of acting, reacting, presenting, writing, and emoting. What they learn in my "playshops" is applicable not just to working in films, commercials, and television. It offers real world experiences that are useful in school, at home, and in the workplace. Looks and gestures can and do speak louder than words. Think before you talk. No amount of apologies can take back a word said in anger or hatred. My motto is "Sticks and stones may break my bones, but words can break my heart."

Communication is the most talked about and least understood area of human behavior. Our ability to communicate in so many modes is unique to humans on earth. There will always be people who know more than you. Listen to them. There will always be people who think they know more than you. Be polite, and listen to them too as it is amazing what you can learn from the least likely people! Always consider the source when evaluating whether to act on the information or not. Sincere communication between parents and their children may be an ideal hardly ever reached; yet it can build trust and strength.

Today I earn my living listening, speaking, interviewing, and communicating. All the practice I got as a young girl has paid dividends beyond my eager imaginings. Communication is your entry to loving relationships, financial wealth, and all that is good in life. Open the gate and walk in.

EXERCISE

Say What You Mean to Say!

How can you adopt strategies to develop a strong loving bond with parents, friends, and co-workers, using the art of communication?

- ★ Show you are giving your full attention by turning off the cell phones and looking into the eyes of your parent or friend.
- ★ Let people finish their sentences without interruptions, corrections, or offering advice.
- ★ Watch your body language.
- ★ Play together.
- ★ Create rituals that are important and personal to you alone, whether it be watching a beautiful sunset, planting a garden, cooking a meal, indulging in a spa treatment, or enjoying a hot cup of chocolate.
- ★ Spend time together to nurture one another's body, mind, and spirit.
- ★ Be one another's head cheerleader. Allow and welcome mistakes. There is no failure, only fertilizer, as long as you learn a lesson.
- ★ Offer compliments while acknowledging competence.

We all have the ability and responsibility to master the art of communication. Cherish the unique gifts of one another and admire the wonder of being. Learning how to communicate when you are young will lead to a lifetime of comprehension and harmony.

☆

"The world is talking. Are you listening?"
Cynthia Brian

The Gift of CURIOSITY

By Sally Franz

When I was four, my grandmother and I were weeding her tulip garden. "Ooo," she squealed with delight. "Look who I found." I looked up and saw she was holding up a lime-green garden snake.

I screamed.

Grandma smiled. "Sally," she said, as she rotated her arms over and over for the snake to continue to his slithering journey, "don't be afraid of something just because you don't understand it. This is my friend Pete. He lives here, and he's much more afraid of you than you are of him. Come closer and look at his spectacular scales. Watch his tongue. Do you know what he is doing? He's smelling you. Isn't that funny? What would we look like if our noses were on the end of our tongues?"

Eventually I dared a touch, and, by the end of the afternoon, the snake and I were more or less pals. Well, at least we were huge curiosities to each other.

As I grew up, curiosity became the best tool I had to face the fear and sadness of not understanding why life was unkind or unfair at times. When people were bullies or cliquish, I pretended I was an anthropologist. I put my hurt feelings aside and became very objective. I'd even get out a notebook and write down: behaviors, language, food, costumes, games, housing, rituals, and pecking order.

Playing Margaret Meade made me stop and realize that when things go wrong it usually has nothing to do with me…or at least I didn't cause it. Observing people rather than being hurt became a very useful tool. But the real test for my anthropology game came fifty years later when I took my youth group on a ski trip. I made sure everyone had a good breakfast, an extra pair of gloves, lunch money, and my cell number in case of an emergency.

Early that morning my left leg started to tingle. The sensation went up to my hip, and, when it started on my right side, I went to get first aide. Within thirty minutes, I was paralyzed from the waist down. I was rushed to a nearby hospital. So much for being an effective leader and being prepared for every possibility.

They found out I had an autoimmune disease, and I was flown in a medevac airplane to my hometown hospital. From there I was taken to a rehabilitation center to learn how to walk again. That was really strange. I was like a toddler banging into doors and walls. But I did it!

Along the way, a lot of people asked me if I was scared or mad at God or the universe. I wasn't. I just kept getting increasingly more curious. Before I knew it, Margaret Meade was in the house. Who are these people? Why do they wear white? What does this strange language mean?

I realized very quickly that if I had spent anytime asking 'Why Me?' I would have literally died using up the energy I needed to survive. This was serious. There was no place for "what ifs", "if only", and "no fair!" There is just so much 'oomph' left inside you when you get really sick, so I chose to use it on getting curious.

And not just about my surroundings. I got very curious about my life's purpose. Here are the questions I asked myself as I lay in the hospital:

★ "What do I have left that I can still use?"

★ "Who will help me?"

★ "Who needs my help?"

★ "What can I do now that I wasn't able to do before?"

★ "What am I learning that is new?"

★ "Who else needs to know about this?"

If you want to survive and thrive, overcome and become…get curious!

EXERCISE

Curiosity Never Killed the Cat

Write about a time when you felt scared, hurt, or left out by a person or group. Now go back in time as an anthropologist and review the scene with your magnifying glass and notebook. Ask these questions:

★ What native group was this person in? (Fourth grade, Scouts, your family
★ What phrases did they use that you found hurtful? (So, as-if, whatever)
★ What clothes did they wear?
★ What food did they eat?
★ What is one positive thing about this group or person?

- Did they have a certain status? (Older, more money, more friends)
- Did they try to use their actions or status to hurt you, subdue you, or ignore you?
- Is this a tribal custom? (Do they act this way to others?)
- If you were to name this person or group of people what name would you give them?
- Are these people different, strange, uneducated, and/or dangerous?
- If "dangerous," how will you protect yourself? (Get help, avoid this tribe)
- If just "different," how will you reach out to them in the future?

☆

"Don't be afraid of something
just because you don't understand it."
Lelia Seelbach (Author's grandmother)

"Curiosity killed the cat,
satisfaction brought him back."
Eugene O'Neill's Diff'rent (1922)

The Gift of DARING

By Rachel Glass

My cousin Victoria and I were at her house in Napa and decided to head out to the vineyard on our bikes. Canadian geese squawked overhead and I felt the cool morning air against my skin as we soared through the grapevines. Soon, it was way too muddy and we had to push the wheels over the mushy, grassy ground. We had almost arrived back to the entrance of the vineyard when we saw a small opening along the edge of the rows that we had never explored before. We parked our bikes and wandered over for a look. It led to the creek surrounding the property. We knew we were *never* to venture into the creek because of poison oak, wild animals, swift currents, and the risk of getting hurt. I thought to myself, we won't get caught, and plus, it would be fun!

We pushed away the blackberry bushes as we slid down the muddy cliff, trying to avoid the poison oak to our left. Clinging to tree branches, we hovered over the cold waters of the dark creek and an island of jagged rocks. Not sure how to traverse the ravine, we both decided to jump across. Screaming, we slipped, falling into the strong current. We tried to stand but our clothes and boots were soaked. We made it to shore, jubilant that we were safe and no one had seen us.

Speedily, we rode home, parked our bicycles, and were walking inside when I noticed something in a basket by the garage—bungee cords. "Maybe we should go back to the creek," I told Victoria, grasping the bungee ropes in my hands. I dangled them in front of her, and she immediately knew what I was thinking. Two minutes later we were back at the opening. Victoria grabbed my ropes, tied them together, and then tied one end to a tree branch. She walked back to our bikes and grabbed our helmets. "Why do we need helmets?" I asked, laughing. "Because the ropes may break" she answered as she propelled down the hill. I grabbed the bungee to descend. "Hurry up!" she yelled. With a loud *snap,* I crashed to the bottom. In shock, I sat on the rocks with Victoria staring at me. She burst out laughing. I caught her laugh attack and lay on the rocks unable to stop cracking up. In this state of giggles, we continued our trek in our secret creek. As we were skipping rocks Victoria suddenly stopped and told me to be quiet. I looked at her, fearing a wild animal was right behind me. She silently whispered in my ear that she heard our moms calling our names.

We were caught! After enduring our mom's rants, I pondered what could have happened to us. As if reading my mind, Victoria said: "What if, when you fell, the water had been deeper and you couldn't get up?" I thought about that and realized how dangerous the situation actually was. The water was extremely cold and with the raging rapids we could have been swept downstream.

The ramifications of our actions hit us like a cold shower. We had not engaged in a daring and fun adventures, but instead had endangered our well being by acting unsafely.

I will never forget the day Victoria and I made our "bungee contraption" but instead of being proud of our actions, what we learned is that we must always think about consequences before doing something daring. Being bold and brave is one thing, being dim and foolhardy is stupidity. Being a teenager offers us the opportunities for excitement and new experiences. I'm always the first to want to explore, navigate, and discover the unknown. It's great to dare to be adventurous and free, however I now know the importance of safety first.

EXERCISE

Dare to Be

Being daring is a positive attribute when you have the courage to step outside your comfort zone and grow. The danger begins when you decide to follow the crowd instead of follow your gut. Here are a few tasks I dare you to experiment with:

- ★ Pick up a musical instrument and learn to play.
- ★ Get a CD of French and begin to *parle français* or be more daring and choose a more exotic foreign language like Swahili.
- ★ Go on a hike and climb a hill that you've never climbed before.
- ★ Try a new, unusual food.
- ★ Decide to tackle a sport you've never played before.

If you do decide to swing across a creek as Victoria and I attempted, make sure you have safety equipment, strong trees, an extra sturdy rope, and a buddy system. Be safe, and you'll always have fun.

☆

"Dare to be yourself but look before your leap."
Rachel Glass

The Gift of DATING

By Cynthia Brian and Heather Brittany

At a traditional English teahouse we frequented whenever we had important issues to discuss, we conceived the idea for our radio segment called T42-A Mother/Daughter Brew. Here we felt free to argue, debate, brainstorm, laugh, and cry. We talked a lot about boys, girls, relationships, differences in dating throughout the generations, and how much it cost teenagers these days to date. While we were talking, we came up with the idea of Dating on a Dime. Dating is part of adolescence, so have a fun and romantic time without breaking the bank.

Cynthia's Bag

When I was in my teens, it was customary for a guy to ask a girl out on a date. Boys always paid. They worked odd jobs to earn the income, or parents would help supplement. It most definitely was expensive buying dinner, movie, and concert tickets, yet it was the fashion of the times. I always wanted to reciprocate in some way so I would bake brownies or host hamburger barbecues, swim parties, and hikes through the hills, as well as teaching the guys to drive our jalopy on our ranch. The Sadie Hawkins dances, named after a man-chasing cartoon character, were always popular. That was the one time in the year when it was socially acceptable for a girl to ask a boy out. Roles were reversed, and the gals paid.

When I moved to Holland after high school, dating was different. Actually, teens didn't date in the Netherlands. We all went out in big groups, and each person paid individually, even if part of a couple. I finally understood what "Dutch treat" meant, and it was empowering. There was never that awkward moment of wondering about etiquette. Each individual contributed his and her share, no questions asked.

Today's teens have caught up with Holland. More and more people go out in groups. And although there is still the occasional freeloader, usually each person pays unless there is a special celebration. It's refreshing to see the affinity between young men and women as they both earn a living and learn to live as equal partners.

Being the budget babe that she is, Heather has come up with a fabulous list of her favorite inexpensive ways to stretch a dollar.

Heather's Bag

Frugal is fun! There is no such thing as a "cheap date" if all your encounters are built around love. With the escalating prices of "fun" and increased financial insecurity, I've outlined romantic, thrilling, and almost—free ways to date on a dime.

My favorites include:

★ **Pack a picnic** and head to a favorite destination. For me, I like to bring brunch, lunch, or dinner, and go to the beach, but a park, the woods, or even your living room floor is just as fun.

★ **Thrift shop hopping** to shop for that used board game. You'll usually find some treasure for less than $2.00, engaging you in many evenings of enjoyment as you discover the rules.

★ **Be a kid at the playground** and slide down the slide and swing on the swings. Don't scare away the kids or get to rowdy, but public parks are for all ages. Enjoy them.

★ **Use your library card** to borrow videos, books on tape, and playful books on puppets, kite flying, or foreign food cookbooks. The card is free, and you'll get lots of ideas for new experiences. What's more romantic than reading poetry to one another?

★ **Go to an author's lecture**, and meet a celebrity. I learned while watching my Mom go on book tours that many book stores schedule frequent presentations be celebrated authors. How terrific is that, to listen to authors read from their book and speak about the writer's journey! You might even get an autograph.

★ **Free concerts in the park** are a blast. In the summer, most cities and towns across America offer a free summer series of concerts. You are encouraged to bring a blanket and a picnic basket while enjoying the music. We always get up and dance—and it's *free*!

★ **Get cultured at a museum**. Many museums have a complimentary entry day every month. Sometimes it's during the week, which offers a special perk for those midweek work blues.

★ **Volunteer together at a charity.** There is nothing better than the feeling that you get from helping others. Whether it's a soup kitchen or a literacy advocacy group, do something meaningful together which will help you appreciate each other and what you already have. Give back and pay it forward.

★ **Karaoke duets!** Hey, everyone can be an American Idol with Karaoke.

Cuddling at home on the couch is cheap, comfy, and cozy, but you can also step out without spending much money. No matter what your age, there are unlimited sources of free or inexpensive entertainment. Theater arts and music majors are required to perform as a graduation requirement, so, if you live near a university, you can watch some terrific performances with a student discount. Become intellectually stimulated while holding hands.

The bottom line is that there is no excuse not to have a great date. A plethora of activities await you if you are willing to seek adventure and romance together.

EXERCISE

Dating on a Dime

Check out your local city magazines for information, ads, coupons, and listings of upcoming events. With the help of the Internet, you can Google the name of an area and find coupons or discounts. Participate as a twosome or as a group. Every person can contribute to the quest by discovering a new activity. And one last suggestion that we highly recommend: call in to your favorite radio station to talk on air. It's totally free, and you may achieve your fifteen minutes of fame. If you want to call in to chat with us, our toll free number is 1-866-613-1612 any Thursday from 3-4PM Pacific time or 6-7PM Eastern time. We're waiting for your call.

☆

"Wishing you romantic days and dreamy evenings.
Be a budget whiz kid, date on a dime!"
Cynthia Brian and Heather Brittany,
The Stella Donna Goddess Gals

The Gift of DESTINY

By Cynthia Brian

"Take 101, Mom, it's scenic and you can stop by my place to see the farm," Justin, a student in San Luis Obispo, exclaimed. "No, take Highway 5, it's ugly, but you'll save four hours," intoned a friend. As Heather's moving day approached, we debated the best driving route from the San Francisco Bay area to San Diego.

It had been an engrossing summer! Heather had turned eighteen, and graduated from high school, events celebrated with numerous parties and festivities. She and I had flown to San Diego several times, rented an apartment, registered for classes, attended Freshman Orientation, walked on the beach, and savored glorious sunsets. On a Mother-Daughter extravaganza, we traveled for two weeks throughout eastern Canada, visiting Montreal, Quebec City, Prince Edward's Island, even Halifax. Bidding farewell to my youngest child would be difficult. As it does for so many parents, the time had arrived to pack Heather's car and drive her to college. After two decades of parenting, my husband and I were emptying our nest.

As part of his plant science and viticulture major, our son, Justin, worked on the farm at Cal Poly University. Because of the five-hour distance, we didn't get to see him often. Although Heather wanted to visit her brother, we were on a tight schedule. After much deliberation and constant mind changing, we opted for the "ugly" route. Those extra few hours would give us a bit more time to get Heather settled into her new abode

By 9:00 AM it was already 90 degrees and promising to be a scorcher as Heather bid adieu to her dad and barnyard animals. At a store in town, we purchased matching rose-colored glasses with small stars embedded in the corners.

Heather was the navigator who calculated the miles traveled by inches driven. We knew that San Diego was approximately 600 miles away, and, by Heather's measurements, the distance was twenty-two inches on the map. Using our mathematical expertise, each inch represented 27.27 miles. Wearing our rose-colored, star-studded glasses, we inched our way south. We called Justin from our cell phone with travel updates as we sang to the tune "Hot, Hot, Hot".

At twelve inches, we made a pit stop in Bakersfield. The cashier sweetly teased us about our matching glasses. "Could I buy your glasses? Customers need them for 'The Grapevine,'" she chuckled.

"The Grapevine" was a dreaded stretch of road just one and three-quarter inches ahead. It's a very steep winding portion of Highway 5 that is notoriously dangerous in the winter months because of black ice, wind, snow, and falling rocks. In the summer months, cars tend to overheat and blow engines with the precipitous climb. I recounted to Heather how in the 1970s my sister Debbie's car had caught fire and burned when she was coming to UCLA to visit me. Our Dad drove all the way from Napa County to rescue her, towing her totally charred car back to our ranch.

It was *really* hot. The thermometer registered 109 as we climbed the grade without air conditioning. Even with our rose-colored glasses, it looked smoggy, hazy, and spooky. "Heather, are we smoking?" I questioned as I strained to look in my side mirrors for any telltale signs.

At that moment, I had a gut sensation that something was wrong with the car. "Something feels funny, Heather".

"There's no smoke, Mom, but pull over. You always told me to pull over and check when you get that gut feeling." Semi trucks and cars zoomed past us as I moved into the farthest right hand lane.

We popped the hood to check the engine. No smoke, but the radiator was empty. I called AAA road service and described our condition. "You've blown either a head gasket or your transmission. In any case, you'll need to be towed on a flat bed truck because your vehicle has four-wheel drive. Are you in a safe place?"

Were we safe? We didn't have a clue, but we had our cell phone. Back home, our friends and neighbors had a mantra whenever anyone needed assistance, be it a skunk in a shed, a rat retrieved from a roof, or a diesel dug from a ditch. An adaptation from the movie *Ghostbusters*, the slogan was "Who you gonna call? "*Justin*" that's who!" Justin never failed to drop everything to help a soul in need. His emergency aid was highly valued and extremely appreciated.

Heather dialed his number on her cell phone. Justin answered. "Hey brother, it's your favorite girls! Our car broke down!"

"Give me the details," he said. Then he instructed us on what to look for in the engine. "You've either blown a head gasket or your transmission. I'm coming to get you."

I looked at our map. "Justin, you're seven inches away from us, that's too far! We already called AAA. They'll tow us to Los Angeles." Justin wanted the car towed to San Luis Obispo so he could repair it. He figured if we were towed to some unknown garage in Los Angeles, we'd end up with a gigantic bill and possibly be stranded in a truly unsafe location.

At that moment, an AAA truck pulled up just as *my* cell phone rang. It was Justin. He wanted to talk to the driver. "Your son wants me to haul you to a meeting place on Highway 56 where he'll pick you up on a flat bed trailer. It's the halfway point." Despite our predicament, Heather and I were in a festive mood. We felt rather playful, as if our rose colored glasses would somehow make a difference.

"How can you two be so happy when your car is kaput, you are traveling 200 miles back the way you just came, and the temperature outside could fry an egg?" the driver asked as we sat in the backseat of his tow truck exchanging quips.

"We have rose colored glasses, and it must be our destiny to see Justin after all!" we giggled.

Highway 56 was the most desolate road we'd ever seen. We drove 3.66 inches and as promised, there, at the arranged intersection, Justin waited with a flat bed trailer and an ice-chest of cold drinks and tasty treats prepared to rescue his girls. Justin had driven over 120 miles to save us. He and the AAA driver moved our battered Explorer to Justin's trailer, we thanked our AAA driver, and off we went on a journey towards the coast. We traveled another 4.4.inches to Justin's barn in San Luis Obispo where he safely parked our vehicle. After a great meal and lots of familial conversation, we showered, then plopped our weary heads on pillows at Justin's house. This detour had been champagne for our souls.

We finally did make it to San Diego in a rented twenty-foot U-Haul truck after twenty-two hours of traveling and several extra inches by taking the slow, "pretty" route. The upside was we were able to visit with our hero, Justin, spending precious time with him as he had originally requested. Heather made it to the university on time for classes, and we learned that things don't always go as planned. Often, something better shows up. Sometimes what seems like an inconvenience or a disaster is a blessing in disguise.

Justin installed a new transmission in Heather's car, saving her the trouble of taking it to a repair shop. The fact that she didn't have a vehicle at college for the first semester was a great way to walk and meet people.

No matter how you plan, destiny intervenes. Roll with the punches. And wear rose-colored glasses.

EXERCISE

Destiny Drivers

Serendipitous opportunities seem to find us when we are making other plans. If you want to predict your future you have to create it yourself. However, keep in mind that you can never push the river. It just flows. The next time something does not go the way you had planned it, take a deep breath, discover the blessing, and seek the beauty. If you have difficulty driving your destiny, buy a pair of rose-colored glasses and live each day the way it comes. When the going gets tough, laugh. Be grateful and know that memories are made of moments like these. Everything can change within a couple of inches. Smile, have fun, be wild, and wacky.

*"There may be something better around the corner.
Wear rose colored glasses to judge your travels
by the smiles, not the miles."*
Cynthia Brian

The Gift of DIFFERENCES

By Anna Myers

The day I learned that I was assigned to a school that was about ninety percent Latino and African American, I started crying. I am a white girl, relatively small, and rather nerdy, and my fashion style tends toward Gothic. I knew that my appearance would make me stand out, and I was absolutely certain that I would be beaten up.

Late that evening, I was wigging out so badly that I had to go outside. What I do when I am stressed out is dance, and I danced barefoot, without a coat, until I got too cold. Just as I stopped dancing, a beautiful shooting star shot across the sky right above me. It truly caught my breath. I made a wish on it that school wouldn't be nearly as bad as I expected. I'm not actually superstitious at all, but just making the wish made me feel tremendously better. I felt a strange sensation of renewed courage, and I even felt warmer.

School was going to begin in a month. I had time to talk to friends about my fears. They advised me to make the best of it. They also advised me to buy less noticeable clothes.

In general, I am outspoken, loud, and eccentric to a fault. However, when the first day of school arrived, I noticed that I was squeaking whenever anyone talked to me. Partly this was because I thought that if I acted timid enough, no one would even notice me enough to want to hurt me. I believe that day at school was the first time that anyone ever told me I was quiet.

By the time sixth period came around, I was shocked to find that not only had I not been beaten up, but also I had made two friends. One guy had even been very heavily flirting with me. He was actually quite cute. My dad greeted me with a great deal of apprehension when I got home and was very surprised to find me grinning. When I told him about my day, he was relieved, that is, until I mentioned being flirted with.

By the end of the second week, I was actually quite popular. I had come out of my formal shell and was acting like my normal insane self. I had a couple of girl friends and a ton of guy friends, was secretary of the school Japanese anime club, and been asked out by a senior. However, being quiet had given me a chance to do a lot of listening, and I had developed a reputation as a good listener, even after my eccentricity returned. My new friends looked to me as someone they could confide in. Many of them had a lot of difficult challenges that they needed to talk about, and knowing how tough they had it gave me respect for them. Being appreciated in school was a new experience for me, since in my previous schools; I had been the lowest rung on the social ladder.

I began to find out about other races, cultures, traditions, fears, and the differences we all share. I learned about the danger and problems that surrounded my classmates. In a school assembly, we were asked how many of us knew someone who had been a victim of gun violence. I was one of only two who did not. Most middle class white people have so little knowledge of the lives of people living around them. The school I am in has the lowest average GPA in the city, but no standardized test could equate the education that I have gained by attending a school of diversity.

One truly defining experience was the day that one of my dear friends at school was arrested for carrying a gun. Someone else had asked him to hold it until school was over so he could "use it for something" after school. My friend should never have agreed to do that. Another acquaintance that is Hispanic, told me what had happened to him a few years earlier. His best friend had brought a gun to school, and my friend was aware of his actions. Unfortunately, my friend did not tell the authorities. His friend used the gun to shoot and kill another person.

These experiences made everything around me suddenly more vivid. I had known that most of the students at my school lived in a different world from me, but this made things more real. Since then, I have learned enough to know that on any day at my school, if every single student was searched, there would be at least one gun, and many, many more knives.

My observations in this new environment have shown me that we all have fears, challenges, and dreams. We just react to situations differently and benefit from different opportunities. While you don't want to change your inner self, it is permissible to make compromises in your outer appearance when you are among people who have a different background or culture As Carl Jung said, "The difference between a good life and a bad life is how you walk through the fire." I think this school experience has prepared me for the fire much more than an education at a homogeneous, elite academy ever could.

EXERCISE

Freak Out

We all experience fears differently. If you feel like you are freaking out, talk to a receptive friend or family member. Clearly explain just what is bothering you, and why. Grabbing a pillow and screaming into it is great. Playing loud music can work wonders. After you feel a few degrees calmer, doing some form of exercise can be a great way to work things out, and it makes you feel stronger physically. Get out of the house and breathe deeply. Go for a few good sprints while listening to a favorite song. I find that when I'm absolutely panicking and freaking out, I get a really big adrenaline rush. Dancing helps me calm down. If you feel hot headed or rash, take a few breaths and exercise before acting irrationally.

The fear of fear is worse than what it is you are afraid of. Deal with your rational fear rationally, and your irrational fear irrationally. Replace your negative yucky thoughts with positive ones.

☆

"Our differences may be
our greatest commonalities.
Face your fears and it disappears."
Cynthia Brian

The Gift of DREAMS

By Cynthia Brian

Do you spend time daydreaming? I sure hope so. Imagine the life you want to live. Are you interested in doing what you love and loving what you do? Do you want to earn-a-living and learn-a-living? You can do and be anything you want in life if you have the courage to dream big enough, be realistic, and do what is necessary to implement those dreams. You can achieve anything in life and make a living doing it when you identify what you want, believe you can get it, and persevere until you have it.

Although parents want what is best for their kids, often parents attempt to decide the life path for their teens. I am always encouraging parents to allow their children to follow their hearts and discover their own career. When we are passionate about an opportunity, we excel.

I was one of those kids always getting in trouble in class because I was talking or asking too many questions. Curious and interested in other people, I found it second nature to understand what made others tick. "Chatty Cathy" would have been a better name for me than Cynthia. The irony is that these early flaws led to my becoming an international speaker earning a living talking by motivating audiences to be the stars they are.

My parents told me that by the time I was three, I was actively performing for aunts, uncles and cousins at weekly Sunday get-togethers. If there weren't people to entertain, I'd dance, sing, and talk to the farm animals. Perhaps it was the applause and giggles that whetted my appetite, but somehow at a young age I always knew I wanted to be an actor. As devout Catholics, this was not what my parents had envisioned for me, so, being an obedient child**,** I then dreamed of becoming a nun.

At eighteen, I flew to Ireland to visit a convent. Despite my interest in a religious life, my first grade teacher, Sister Mary Germaine suggested that I was better suited for the bright lights of Hollywood. Thank goodness she understood my passions. Just think how I would have tormented those holy souls with my singing, dancing, antics, and talking.

Just because you have a dream, it doesn't mean it will come true without hard work. Norman Vincent Peale said, "Nothing of great value in life comes easily. The things of highest value sometimes come hard. The gold that has the greatest value lies deepest in the earth, as do the diamonds." Happiness is doing what you love and loving what you do. The bigger your dream, the brighter your future. Here are the steps I teach to living your dreams.

- ★ **Dream the Dream:** If you don't already know what your dream is, the best way to find out is to brainstorm what you love in life. What are you really, really, really good at? What do you love to do? If you knew you couldn't fail, what would you try?
- ★ **Write the Plan:** Write everything down on paper. You can't get where you want to get unless you know where you are going. You must consider ways you can create the reality of your dream. Make a list of what you will need to do, where you will need to go, and how you will do it.
- ★ **Get the Skills:** Talent and skills are different. Everyone is born with innate talents but skills are learned and developed. Get educated, take a class, find the mentor, hire a coach, learn your trade. Then you can blend your talent with your new skills.
- ★ **Go into Action:** It's up to you to make "it" happen. Don 't expect your doorbell to ring with the offer of a lifetime. You'll need to pound the pavement, send out résumés, proposals, and manuscripts. Join organizations that may need your services, network with everyone you know, talk to people, ask for help, and share your dream.
- ★ **Find Support:** Surround yourself with people who support your desires and believe in your ability to prevail. Just one person is enough to start with. Hire a coach who will be your greatest advocate. You need a champion you can depend on. No one ever succeeds alone.
- ★ **Believe in Yourself:** No plan can prosper if you lack faith in yourself.

Trust in yourself and all the possibilities the universe offers. Conceive, believe, achieve. You can *be* and *do.*

Once you have developed your plan, stop worrying about things you can't control. Work hard. Don't be attached to pre-conceived outcomes, because sometimes detours in your progress result in the greatest achievements. Be flexible. Remember to enjoy the moment. You have a dream and you have a strategy. Now follow it.

EXERCISE

Dream Big

This questionnaire is designed to help you discover your dreams, identify your fears, and get you moving in the right direction. Answer truthfully and spontaneously. Nothing is too outrageous. Just write down what you feel, want, need, and desire, no matter how silly you think it may be. Let's make your dreams come true.

- ★ What motivates you to get out of bed in the morning?
- ★ If you were told you had years to live, how would you spend your days?
- ★ If there were no limitations, including, money, skills, education, or family obligations, what would be your ultimate passion to pursue in this lifetime?
- ★ List your favorite hobbies or leisure time activities...things that make you lose track of time.
- ★ Name people who love and support you. You can count on these people 100 percent.
- ★ Do you have a mentor, and, if so, who and why?
- ★ What do you fear?
- ★ List all your dreams, no matter how small, that have been realized.
- ★ Do you easily get discouraged? If so, why?
- ★ Do you take time to daydream, meditate, or contemplate the future, or do you feel this is a waste of time? Describe your feelings and list your dreams.
- ★ What and who do you want to be when you grow up?

Take it one day at time. Don't worry, don't look for results, allow dreams to happen. One day the puzzle will be put together, and you'll be living your dreams.

☆

"Dream it! Do it!"
Cynthia Brian

The Gift of EDUCATION

By Dr. Don Martin

My early years unfolded in a very sheltered world where thinking, questioning, taking an opposing view, and intellectual stimulation were not valued or encouraged. In fact, these gifts were considered suspect. After graduating from high school, my next step was dictated to me, as it was to my siblings. We had to spend at least one year enrolled in a Bible school. Sadly, none of my siblings ever graduated from college. Thankfully, I did earn my bachelor's degree, even though my undergraduate experience was greatly lacking in terms of exposure to a broad liberal arts education.

As my senior year of college approached, it was clear that moving away from the sheltered environment of my youth was necessary. Knowing very little about the incredible educational options available to me, I applied to the only graduate school to come to my attention during college. Much to my amazement, this institution offered me admission. One of my parents tried to talk me out of going. If anything, my commitment to pursue my educational goals only increased. In the end, it was my great honor to earn a master's in Communications from Wheaton College and a doctoral degree in Higher Education Administration from Northwestern University. My life has been enriched beyond belief as a result.

While pursing my doctoral degree, life's path took a very dark turn. My marriage unexpectedly came to an end. In addition, interactions with my family became strained beyond repair as I moved away from many of the beliefs that had been forced upon me in years gone by. There were times it seemed that my path was taking me though a continuous dark tunnel with no end in sight. But the light did shine again. With the help of some key influencers, a personal faith that was solely mine, and an unwillingness to give up, things eventually came together in every area of my life.

Should you wish to pursue an education, do not let anyone or anything stand in your way. You have already read about the personal and family crises that unfolded during the pursuit of my doctoral degree. Let me share another "test" of my commitment: My first response from the institution to which I'd applied was a denial letter. This was extremely disappointing. After a few days of cooling off, I placed a phone call to the admissions office, asking if it would be possible to get some feedback on my application. Upon hearing this feedback, it became clear that only one of the first two GRE test scores had been placed in my file. I asked if I could provide the second set of scores, and was told yes. An additional letter of recommendation focusing on my academic skills was also requested. Both were immediately provided to the admissions office. Within a month, this same institution admitted me. Not only that, they reduced the number of courses required for my program of study from twenty-seven to eighteen. This was like already having completed one year of study before enrolling.

Education is truly a gift–in many ways a gift to yourself. It is an investment that always provides a wonderful return, including financial gains. The requirements for fulfilling your educational goals are only two: Persistence and Determination. Contrary to what many think, getting an education is affordable, can be accomplished at any age, does not require that you have a high IQ, and reaps huge benefits even if you do not attend one of the top ranked institutions. If I can earn an undergraduate and graduate degree, anyone can. That means ***you!***

EXERCISE

Persistence Prevails

Take a sheet of paper and write down all the obstacles you believe are holding you back from pursuing your educational goals and dreams. Then place either the word "persistence" or "determination" beside each item. This will be your guide to show how you will overcome the obstacles you believe lie in your path. As you have just read, persistence and determination are nearly invincible. If you want to get an education, *you can.*

☆

"Nothing in this world can take the place of persistence. Talent will not: nothing is more common than unsuccessful people with talent. Genius will not; unrewarded genius is almost a proverb. Education will not; the world is full of educated derelicts. Persistence and determination alone are omnipotent. The slogan 'press on' has solved and always will solve the problems of the human race."

Calvin Coolidge,
Thirtieth President of the United States, 1872-1933

The Gift of ENCOURAGEMENT

By BilliJo Doll

When I was in school, I knew people by their shoes. Some of my classmates thought this was funny and would have contests asking me who someone was by looking at their shoes. The only time I was wrong was when someone wore new shoes to school.

One time as I walked down the crowded hall, books clutched to my chest, someone said "Hi" to me. I looked up and ran into the heat radiator. My books and papers all fell to the floor—right in front of the boys' lavatory. As I tried to pick up my things, other students kicked them around the hall. It was one of the more embarrassing moments of my life.

My life changed from looking down at shoes to looking up because of special mentors who took the time to encourage me. In my 20's, I participated in-group counseling. The counselor, Bill, asked all of us to bring a list of twenty goals. I worked diligently on this assignment, but could only come up with ten things that I thought I could accomplish in my life. When I turned in my project, he gave it back to me stating, "I said twenty." I felt hurt and angry. Admittedly, I copped an attitude and wrote down ten more things that I knew were totally impossible for me ever to achieve.

Five years later, I discovered that list in a desk drawer. Of the twenty items on the list, I had accomplished more of the "impossible" ten than I had of the "doable" ten. I had become a college student, danced on stage in front of hundreds of people, gone snorkeling, sailed on a cruise ship, and become a published writer with an article in a magazine.

I was a "mistress-of-ceremonies" for a banquet before I found the courage to go to college. I was scared to death. I did not feel comfortable telling jokes as many emcees do, so I wrote a ballad and read it. In the audience was a professor emeritus named Jack. Afterward; he asked if I were a student of Wallace Stegner and requested a copy of the ballad. His simple, less-than-five-minute conversation gave me the courage to attempt college. While in school, Jack and I would have coffee, and he continued to encourage me.

One day my ecology professor, Bret, summoned me to his office. I wondered why I was in trouble. Instead, he took out a paper I had written and said, "I think you have a gift. If you would like, I am willing to work with you to improve your writing." Then my advisor, Clayton, hired me to help graduate students on their projects. He encouraged me more than probably any other one individual.

After a successful, albeit short, career in my chosen field, I became ill and had to retire. For years I was housebound with a horrid virus that attacked my immune system. It was during that time I began to write novels. I have read that only one novel in a thousand gets published. Because I had learned to believe in myself, I mailed my manuscripts, and, despite numerous rejection notices, I never stopped pitching my work until I was offered my first book contract. Through speaking about my struggles and my writing, I was booked to host a radio show, Coping with Life.

Encouragement is support and positive urging. To encourage means to give someone else courage. I have been able to accomplish my goals because of the people who believed in me and in my abilities. They took the time and the effort to offer me the gift of encouragement. Welcome encouragement into your life and foster it in others.

EXERCISE

Encouragement Mint

The Gift of Encouragement begins with kindness and caring.

★ Close your eyes and think of ways to encourage the people in your life.
★ Compliment someone every day.
★ Practice saying: "Yes, I believe you can do it."
★ Look for ways and times to tell people good things about themselves.
★ Try to get creative with ways to encourage.
★ Do not give up on your own dreams.
★ Help someone achieve her dreams.
★ Write a list of ten doable and ten impossible dreams. (Hide the list for a couple of years.)

When you decide to do your best every day, your life will be filled with unexpected encouragement and joy.

"Flatter me, and I may not believe you.
Criticize me, and I may not like you.
Ignore me, and I may not forgive you.
Encourage me, and I may not forget you."
William Arthur

The Gift of FAITH

By Dani Wong

I'd like to tell you about my dad. Imagine talking to the person you admire most. Everything is perfect. Nothing can go wrong. He encourages you to achieve, to be a "go-getter" in life. When something is wrong, he makes you feel better. It's almost unreal how this person can turn your feelings around. Now stop.

The next thing you know, that person is gone. The fuel that powered your very purpose is stalled. The weird thing is, his body is still there. Nothing is the same. You can gaze into his eyes, searching for an answer. But he cannot speak. It seems he may be lost forever. Where is faith when you need it most?

When I was fifteen, my dad had a stroke.

My dad was away on a business trip, and I missed him terribly. We always had great times together. He taught me how to throw a football and took me swimming in the rain. That day, when my mom picked him up from the airport, he was not himself. He was too tired to do anything. This was odd, considering he was the fittest person I knew. He worked out everyday and had the ability to do endless push-ups. That night, my dad went right to bed. I accepted this reluctantly, but resolved that we would talk in the morning. It never happened.

My mom rushed my dad to the emergency room after he started struggling to form words and no longer had control of his right arm or leg. The doctors said that my dad was the victim of a severe stroke. I couldn't believe what I was hearing. No, this couldn't have happened, not to *my dad*. Not to the man who had a million friends, was kind to everyone, and was a brilliant father. But it did. I found myself in a deep state of confusion, filled with despair.

How could I go on seeing him like this? He couldn't even talk to me. I soon realized that our long conversations were history. I stared at his silent, motionless body. It was at that moment that I finally understood the phrase "Everything can change in an instant." The week before, my dad was healthy and strong. Now he was lying in a hospital bed, unable to move his right side or talk. Tears became a constant instead of a rarity. I hated crying, but I couldn't help it. How difficult it was to going through such a traumatic experience as a teenager! These things aren't supposed to happen when we are so young. The pressure was enormous. It was challenging to focus on school while coping with this heartache. The hardest part of everything was that my own father, the man who taught me to live and dream, couldn't even say, "I love you." I had to have faith that he would recover.

Zoom ahead one year. Although our lives are not perfect, my dad's health has improved tremendously. We found therapy programs for my dad, and he was extremely motivated to get back onto his feet. He went through intensive neuro-rehab, and within two months, he started walking again. The physical and speech therapy programs are influencing his recovery. Although everyday is a challenge, we have faith that with love and support he can accomplish anything. His goal is to fully restore his health.

Through these difficult times, I am not alone. My mom, sister, and I are facing the challenges together. We know that we have a hard journey ahead of us, but we love my dad so much that we'll do anything to help him. I also am so fortunate to have an extended family and friends to support me. I don't know what I'd do without them.

Sometimes the only thing you have to hang onto is faith. You cling onto it like a lifejacket in the middle of the ocean. Faith is not something you can touch, but you can feel it all around you. Faith helps you sail through the storms of life when the waves swell so high that you are sure you'll drown. We believe in my dad's ability to recover. His conviction that he will heal boosts our trust in his resilience. Dad has faith in himself and we have faith in him.

Faith takes courage and determination to make the impossible possible. In life, faith helps us overcome the biggest obstacles.

EXERCISE

Keep the Faith

We all go through tough situations. Whether you've lost someone close to you or you are completely stressed out, it's easy to feel discouraged. The following technique can help you feel better when things aren't going so well. You have sent letters to your relatives and friends, but have you ever sent one to yourself? It is actually a very effective way to pinpoint what's bothering you and to make yourself feel better.

- ★ Start by writing a letter to yourself. Don't worry about grammar, spelling, or even how it sounds. Remember, this is for your eyes only.
- ★ Write everything down that's going through your head. Pour out your emotions and really express how you feel. You can jot down everything that's worrying you or things you miss about a loved one.
- ★ Now that everything is on paper, it's time to put it away. Seal the letter and put it in a safe place.
- ★ When you are having a good day and feel a little more positive, pull out the letter. It's time to have faith. Know that even though it may not seem like it, things will get better. It may sound cliché, but it's true. Look at the letter and think about what you wrote down. Come to terms with why you felt this way.

Now, have faith that things will improve. With time, it will be easier to accept the past and look forward to your future.

☆

"Faith invigorates our souls,
energizes our minds,
and shapes our dreams."
Dani Wong

The Gift of
FINANCIAL LITERACY

By Heather Brittany

Kids don't need allowances. At eight years old, you're not paying a mortgage or filling the car up with gas, so your biggest decision is choosing between Frosted Flakes or Coco Pebbles. Children may not need allowances, but they do need a financial education.

Growing up, we had chores. Lots and lots of chores. Anything from vacuuming the house and cleaning toilets to feeding the goats, mucking the barn, pulling weeds, and mowing the lawns. My mom treated these daily tasks as our childhood occupation. An allowance was not part of our vocabulary. We were a component of a family, and each member shared in the duties of enjoying a home. Mom was teaching us lessons in the value of work and self-sufficiency.

Childhood chores are a great simulation for living in the real world. Our parents supplied all the necessities for school and daily living. We had to work for the extras. Instead of paying us for our household tasks, mom created a point system. We made a list of all the things we really wanted, then attached a number of points needed to attain each item. We listed prizes great and small: movies, backpacks, special meals, rollerblades, bicycles, rollerblades, skateboards, train sets, skis, or trips to Disneyland and Universal Studios. When we saved enough points, we were able to "cash in" for an item with that number of points. On a bulletin board in the pantry, our points were tallied each week. Mom was teaching us that if we worked diligently without complaint, we would earn our own money. And if we saved it, eventually we would be able to afford something grand.

My brother and I saved many of our hard earned points for five years. Then one day we cashed in our investment for a giant professional trampoline. To a child, buying a full-scale trampoline is comparable to an adult buying a first car or house. It felt amazing! Though it took five years to save enough points, it was worth the wait. It taught us invaluable money-saving skills and, more important the value of having a work ethic.

I took this knowledge into my teen years, and, as soon as I was allowed a work permit, I got a job. I opened a savings account at the local bank where I deposited my bi-weekly paychecks. It felt really good not having to ask my parents for money when I wanted something. It also felt really good that I had ownership of certain items because I had earned the money to buy them myself.

By the time I went to university, I had almost saved enough money to fund my college education independently. I applied for part time jobs and continued to work to supplement my simple lifestyle. Research suggests that students who work at least fifteen hours per week actually do better in school than peers who don't have a job. And even though it is tough at times to juggle both work and school, and the government takes a big chunk of my salary, I always felt proud-knowing that I am capable of being self-supporting.

I budget and prioritize purchases. Making my own living teaches me responsibility and offers a sense of achievement. Taking advantage of coupons and discounts stretches my meager wages. So many young people I know feel entitled to money and possessions and expect their parents to foot the bill. It may have begun with receiving an allowance for not having to do anything. To me, that is not a good model for success.

It would be great to think that money and all the challenges it brings are not important, but most decisions we make are in fact centered on our finances. Not a day goes by when we are not called upon to understand basic math. Are you learning the arithmetic you need to survive in the world? No one in my high school ever explained how credit cards worked or how a person attains good credit or defaults with bad credit. How about you? It may be time to go back to basics to educate yourself to become financially literate. Money matters.

My mom started working and saving when she was a child, and she instilled the same kind of ethics in me. Although I still have much to learn, I am on my way to being financially independent because of the skills I garnered as a child working on a point system. Over the years, my brother and I earned everything on our list. Today we are grateful that the money we have accrued has arrived the old fashioned way-we earned it.

EXERCISE

Dollar Signs

Talk with your parents about opening a savings account for you. Don't ask for or expect an allowance. Instead offer to earn your dollars with specific chores. Take up babysitting, gardening, dog walking, sign making, or small jobs around the house or in your neighborhood. Deposit a minimum of 75 percent of what you earn in your savings account. Clip coupons and write a budget. Start your financial education today. Learn as much as possible about investing in your future. It's never too early or too late to start saving. You'll have the satisfaction of independence and develop a work ethic that will take you far in life.

☆

"A penny saved is a penny earned."
Benjamin Franklin "

"Save today, spend tomorrow."
Heather Brittany

The Gift of FORGIVENESS

By Steve Mitchell

My very good friend was six years old and very lost. His dad had left when he was two years old. Although he didn't understand why his heart felt as if it had a giant hole in the middle, he knew that *something* was missing. The concept of a traditional two-parent family was foreign to him. Although today single-parent families are predominate in the population, when he was a boy divorce was not prevalent. When he visited friends who had "real" families, he felt ashamed to admit that he only had one parent.

Later in his life, he told his story to me. I was intrigued and began to ask many questions so I could truly understand his experience. Perhaps I could help. He described a feeling of emptiness, shame, and confusion. He thought it was his fault that he did not have a dad. When I asked how a six-year old could truly understand what "shame" meant, he suddenly looked away from me and thought for a long while. With tears in his eyes, he said, "I do not know how a six-year old could understand what shame truly means, but I can tell you this. If there was a way I could go back in time to hold that little boy until his shame finally went away, I would do it, no matter how long it took."

That little lost six-year old was I.

When I went back to heal his pain, he taught me two secrets, timeless treasures that I wish to share with you. The first is that children are never the cause of a divorce. Ever. If you are faced with parents who no longer choose to live together, remember that you did not cause their separation. If they are mentally healthy adults who desire to be excellent parents, they are both devastated that they may have failed you. And the second secret is that we need to forgive. To forgive means to accept that something bad has happened, and then to let go of the emotional pain associated with it.

When you forgive someone, it is not about them hurting you and you "letting go of your resentment" or "letting him or her off the hook". The act of forgiveness really benefits the person who does the forgiving, not those who are forgiven. It allows us to let go of the emotional hurts.

Forgiveness requires strength of character. It takes courage. Why does it always seem that bigger, healthier, happier, cooler, and most impressive person forgives first?

EXERCISE

Forgive Your Enemies

Start by picking one person who has made you mad. Has someone hurt you, ridiculed you, made you jealous, cut you off in traffic, or spilled hot coffee on your lap? Finding someone to forgive is easy. Hold an image of this person closely in your thoughts, *see them, feel them, and let them in.* In your mind's eye, see them being successful, see them smiling, *know* they are happy and content, be happy for them, and give them all of your love. Then give them more. Create a colorful, vibrant, and clear picture of them enjoying a wonderful life, laughing, and enriched with love.

Don't question it—do it. If it doesn't come easily, work harder to keep it up. Then begin to notice how your feelings change. You may feel lighter. You may surprisingly see them very differently. It doesn't matter what happens. Keep showering your offenders with love and light.

Once you get good at this "seek and shower with love" practice, it's time to dig deeper to find those sentiments of anger or hurt that are buried in your past. Repeat your positive treatment. Most important, find the one person in your life who needs your love and forgiveness more than any other, probably your number one enemy—yourself. We must learn to forgive ourselves and forge ahead. You get the picture. Imagine yourself being loved, successful, happy, and joyful. Feel, smell, taste, and experience total absolution. Allow yourself to be embraced by love. Get creative. Breathe and see yourself with everything you could possibly want. Be the first to forgive. Finally, don't forget to thank that six-year old inside of you!

☆

"The weak can never forgive;
forgiveness is the attribute of the strong."
Mahatma Gandhi

The Gift of FORTITUDE

By Cynthia Brian

What do you say to a daughter who is turned down by the college of her choice and won't take "no" for an answer—five times!

Meet Heather Brittany, who, as a vivacious seventeen-year-old high school senior, believed in herself and all her possibilities. At age four, she endured arduous surgery to save her life. I spent two weeks camping by her bedside, calling it "our special adventure," and indeed it secured a mother/daughter bond that has not been broken.

At a very early age, Heather decided that when she went off to college, she would take along Mommy and Halloween, her cat. By age seven, Heather was diagnosed with learning disabilities and placed in a special program. Instead of viewing herself as challenged, she chose to see herself as a "special star." Although she struggled with her studies, she excelled in athletics, drama, and her work with animals.

By eighth grade, Heather was a straight "A" student, assisting other learning-disabled children to overcome their obstacles. Then, much to her apprehensive delight, the school administrators disqualified Heather from the special resource program and returned her to regular classes. She knew that high school would offer numerous challenges, and she was right. She soon faltered. Her grades fell to "C's" and "D's" because she couldn't' master the art of test taking. She pleaded for re-admittance to the learning-disabled program, but her application was denied. Heather was told that she needed to fail and get straight "F's" before she could qualify.

Failure is not part of Heather's vocabulary, so she sought outside help. College admission was foremost in her mind. She had to work harder than all her friends, but she was determined to get top grades while remaining involved in the many activities she felt were important to being a well-rounded individual. Her hours were filled with leadership responsibilities, including the 4-H club, church, charities, her menagerie of adopted animals, and volunteer work. As her constant cheerleader and motivator, I scheduled weekly "tea times" to strategize options. We pasted positive quotations on the walls of her bedroom to inspire her to greatness, and together we visited college campuses so Heather could review her future selections.

Heather fell in love with a university in San Diego. By her senior year, her high school grade point average was a solid 3.5. She was confident she would be accepted. Instead, she received a rejection letter. *Rejection number one!* She immediately phoned the Admissions Office to ask about the appeal process. "This year there is no appeal process," she was told. "We had 45,000 applications for 5,000 slots. We're sorry. We can forward your application to another school." *Rejection number two!*

But Heather didn't want another school. Her dream was San Diego, and I encouraged her to imagine her reality, reach for the stars, and expect to land on them. Heather reasoned that the school just didn't understand her potential or know her as a person. There was no way she was giving up now. She looked at the quotations she lived by plastered on her bedroom walls. Her strength and fortitude pressed on. She could write memorable essays, create outstanding projects, and perform at the highest levels in verbal examinations, although she had not mastered taking tests in school. Now she was confronting the biggest test of all.

"Never, never, never give up," Winston Churchill had said. "We must either find a way, or make one," said Hannibal when he crossed the uncrossable Alps. Heather was determined to design her own future. But how?

She put together a formal appeal to the Admissions Office. She gathered her most recent school transcripts and got even more glowing letters of recommendation from her teachers, counselors, talent agent, principal, and community leaders. So many letters arrived that they couldn't all be submitted. Then she made a video highlighting her acting and communication skills. This impressive PR package was sent off to the Admissions Office. Again, Heather was certain that this time they'd "see Heather, the person, not just a number." Acceptance was just days away.

When a reply arrived from the college, she eagerly tore open the envelope. It was a duplicate of her first rejection letter. *Rejection number three!*

Most kids would have given up. Not Heather! Rejection was nothing new. After all, she had been acting and modeling in TV and film since she was a baby. Instead of "being sensible," she picked up the phone and called the Admissions Office again. A special orientation day was approaching for admitted students, and she wanted to attend. "The event is only for our admitted freshman," she was told. "I'm sorry, but you are not one of them." *Rejection number four!*

So, did Heather finally give up? Heather had staying power. She kept talking, using all her best communication and persuasion skills. Finally, the Administration Office wearily said she would not be barred if she showed up. With me in tow, Heather traveled to San Diego and introduced herself and her situation to everyone she met. She persuaded faculty members to support her and endorse her efforts. Her persistence, determination, stamina, and fortitude in the face of defeat were spectacular. After her journey, she followed up with thank-you notes, e-mails, and personal calls to everyone she had met.

Another letter arrived. Again, she had been denied. *Rejection number five*! Surely any sensible person would have acknowledged defeat.

Not endurance Heather. She immediately contacted the chair of her declared major and asked for help. By this time, the Department of Theatre Arts had recognized her unquenchable enthusiasm and sense of purpose, traits essential for success in the entertainment world. Although they couldn't guarantee admission, they could recruit one person and they decided to recruit her. They supported her admissions appeal and assured the University that they would be responsible for tracking her progress, mentoring her, and helping her exceed the University's standards. Heather had found her champion. But would the Admissions Office find her worthy?

On April 15, Heather opened the envelope containing her latest high school grades. She now had a 3.67 grade point average, plus numerous outstanding teenager awards. Still, she had received no college admittance letter. At last, her vision started to waiver. "Mom, I have total faith that I deserve to be admitted. I know I will add value to their campus, but I'm getting discouraged. How much longer can I hold on?"

"Honey," I responded, "Persevere. No matter what happens, you are already a star."

At 2 pm on April 16, the phone rang. "She's ours! She is all ours!" screamed an excited voice. The co-chair of the Department of Theatre Arts had just been notified that Heather was finally accepted. It took more than an hour to get the news to Heather who was still at school taking yet another test. I finally reached her by phone. "Heather, you did it! You're in!" I shouted between sobs. Heather responded, " No, Mom, we did it! We're going to college!"

Heather was rejected *five* times in forty-five days. Any sensible person would have given up. Not Heather. She was tenacious, determined, and passionate about her abilities. She never lost sight of her dream. It was the best Mother's Day ever because that fall, Heather and I went to college.

Fortitude is the will to succeed despite the odds. Fortitude is the stamina to keep on going even when the going is rough. When you are resolved to find a way with purpose and passion, you will discover the strength to build a path where none existed before. Never give up on your dreams. Stay the course.

EXERCISE

True Grit

When every sign tells you to stop, it's difficult to keep going. Yet, when you believe in yourself and know in the depths of your soul that you are on the right path, you must listen to your inner voice. What is it you want to accomplish more than anything despite the naysayers and advice to the contrary? Determine to succeed, get the skills you need, go into action, ask for help, have faith in your abilities, and allow God and the universe to open the doors. Sometimes the person who wins is the one who hung in there the longest. Like our friend Dr. Bernie Siegel says, "hoping means seeing that the outcome you want is possible, then working for it." Fortitude is staying power. Endure. Persevere. Pray. Persist. Have the guts for true grit. No matter what happens, you are already a star.

☆

"Tell me 'no' then watch me go!"
Heather Brittany

The Gift of FREEDOM

By Cynthia Brian

The Iron Curtain...although it was daunting in 1972, still I longed to visit the USSR. Revered acting directors Stanislavsky and Chekhov had been members of the Moscow Art Theatre, and their contributions to "the method" and experimental techniques in acting intrigued me. Then there were the Russian Ballet, the Russian circus, and the Russian gymnasts. All had perfected their art forms to the four qualities of artist creation: ease, form, beauty, and entirety.

My opportunity finally came when I was living in France during 1971-72. A two-month study program was announced that included meeting and working with the artistic community in Latvia, the USSR, and Poland. I signed up at once.

The trip turned out not to be a lesson in freedom of expression as I soon found out, but a study of manipulation and indoctrination. The United States at the time was involved in the Vietnam War, a full-fledged, undeclared atrocity that was killing young Americans and scarring the minds and emotions of those who survived. Although I loved America, I was against what we were doing in Southeast Asia. Like many teenagers at the time, I believed it was unfair to require young people to die for their country before they were allowed to vote. Many Americans were loudly protesting our government's policies; a luxury that I soon learned was unavailable behind the Iron Curtain.

Our plane landed in Leningrad, and we all went to claim our baggage. I had covered my backpack with small flags, mementos of each nation I had visited on my journey. But when I retrieved my luggage, all the flags of the non-Communist countries had been cut off. Whether someone had taken them as souvenirs of countries they had little chance of visiting or an official had cut them off for political reasons, I never knew.

We were taken to a holding room where we were searched by armed guards. Two of my fellow students had made the mistake of taking a photograph in the airport. They were quickly arrested and taken away as spies, their cameras, and film confiscated. When they were returned to the group two days later, they were exhausted and bedraggled from intensive interrogation.

Our polite but timid tour guide collected our passports "for safe keeping." Actually, the authorities feared we might sell them to local citizens, then claim they were lost and apply for new ones at an American embassy. We were told we must convert a specific amount of cash into rubles at the official moneychangers and spend it all. No giving money away, and anyone getting the much more favorable exchange rate from black marketeers would be severely punished. Actually, it hardly mattered. We soon found there was nothing to buy with our rubles except propaganda posters, Lenin buttons, those stacking Russian dolls, and vodka.

In the USSR, where the Russian Revolution had ousted the Czar in 1917 and installed a communist regime, few residents remained who remembered a country called Russia. Not that life under the Czars could be called freedom, but at least art, music, and beauty had been encouraged. The only beauty I now witnessed was pre-1917. Now, the cities were gray, the sky was gray, the clothing was gray, the sugary tea was gray. Life was dismal and gray. Life under Soviet rule was completely colorless. People cued in long lines for everything. Everyone appeared forlorn and beaten down. It was apparent that anything pleasurable was forbidden to the common citizen, perhaps except the opera and ballet, which were fully subsidized companies. The streets were in utter disrepair, with potholes and crumbling curbsides plaguing the roadways. The multi-story, block apartment buildings were unadorned and absent of color, except for the gray laundry hanging from windows. In this land of the proletariat working class, gray was the national color. A couple of times, I witnessed a welcome flash of a fuchsia babushka, perhaps a nod of rebellion towards the grim living conditions. I began to loathe gray.

My fantasy of artists working in harmony and with a free spirit was quickly crushed. We went to the museums, circuses, theater, ballet, and gymnastic competitions, but the happy exchange of artistic ideas was nonexistent. The artists could speak to us only in hushed tones when the attention of our tour guides was elsewhere. As they spoke, their eyes rarely met ours as they scanned the area for any clandestine agents. They were eager to know what we knew, and what it was like where we came from. What were the popular songs, films, plays? How did a hamburger taste? I felt a strong sadness and a sense of them being prisoners of time. Yet, their instinctive freedom was expressed in their creativity, their internal beauty, and their art forms.

One day, as I was walking in the rain, I found a huge rusty broken padlock on the ground. I picked it up, and, instinctively looking around to see if anyone was looking, hid it in my coat. This, I decided, would be the memento to remind me of the value of my own freedom.

When we reached Latvia and Poland, the atmosphere changed. These countries had only recently been annexed by the Soviet Union, and some people could remember a time before World War II when life was different. Everything was more colorful, and people still had some spunk in them. Confrontations between citizens and police occurred regularly in the streets, and black market trading was brisk. I had the feeling that these people would die to restore their freedom. Latvians and Poles were openly friendly to us, asking many questions. Remember that in the 1970's, it was forbidden for them to see Western films or magazines. Information crossed the borders only via the Black Market. (I even got offers to buy my passport, backpack, and clothes.) The energy exuded from the citizens in these countries indicated a great desire for more personal freedom. I got quite chummy with our tour guide and gave her a pair of my Levi's when I left. To her, they were a priceless gift, a symbol of hope for the future. She secretly begged me to write her and to send her a bottle of French perfume. I shipped a parcel as soon as I returned to France. Just as my flags had been ripped off my backpack, the perfume was stolen from the package. I received several letters from her, all with parts cut out. The last one read, "In my dreams I am a butterfly." She had achieved freedom, if only in her mind.

After two months behind the "Iron Curtain," I knew how appropriate the name was. It was impenetrable. Human emotions and ambitions were crushed in the name of an ideal. Life might have been egalitarian, but it was miserable, merely a meager existence. Most citizens performed the jobs they were assigned at preset wages and could not move around or leave the country.

The dissolution of the old Soviet Union has brought a sort of "democracy," one fraught with crime, corruption, violence, and starvation. It will take time for the government and its people to work out a system of equality and freedoms, but at least it is a beginning.

There are countries all over the world that hold their citizens hostage, repress women and children, sanction slavery, and don't allow freedom of religion and expression. People are still persecuted on ethnic issues, and many people are denied a basic education. The fabric of civilization is so fragile.

When I returned to America, the first thing I did was kiss the ground. Those two months behind the Iron Curtain felt like years, and there were moments when I was not sure I would make it back home. But I had kept my personal freedom alive in my imagination, and that's the lesson I brought back. Since then, I have become very good friends with several people, now American citizens, who grew up in Communist countries. They love their heritage, their faraway families, their culture, and are nostalgic for their country. They are also grateful to be living in America, a land of opportunity and personal freedom.

Perhaps no one is ever truly free on every level. No matter what our circumstances, though, we can hold the illusion of independence when we believe we are free. The ugliest caterpillar can dream of the day when it will be a butterfly.

I appreciate the complexities of the gift of freedom. America may not be perfect—no country is. America is great because it is a work-in-progress, a country constantly struggling to balance rights with responsibilities and to maintain a level of freedom and justice for all. I feel fortunate to have had the opportunity to be born in a land that allows me the ability to travel the world, witnessing the cultures and lifestyles of other nations, and then to return to a country that welcomes my self-expression. Yes, I am proud to be an American! The rusty padlock stands guard on my desk as my reminder that freedom is never free.

EXERCISE

Butterflies Are Free

Having even a limited sense of autonomy is better than having none at all. Studies of prisoners of war indicate that those who never lost hope under the most brutal conditions did so by focusing on internal freedom. In difficult situations, mental and spiritual freedom may be your only options.

Here is an exercise I give my students to help them visualize a life of release. Imagine a butterfly is landing on your open palm. Admire the beauty, the fine details of the wings. Feel the way it tickles your hand with its wings. Stand quietly and see this magnificent creature, knowing that not long ago it was trapped in a cocoon. Let the butterfly symbolize all your unmet wants, needs, and desires. Mourn for the sadness you have known and for the times you have felt locked up in a world of misunderstanding. Now watch the butterfly fly away and feel the exhilaration of letting go of your own trepidations. Release fear, and breathe in freedom.

☆

"Freedom in never free.
Believe you are free,
and your chains will be broken."
Cynthia Brian

The Gift of FRIENDS

By Erica Miner

"Jessica Rowe knew how different she was from her three best friends, but she never imagined how desperately they needed each other. Yet, as she was about to discover, that was all part of growing up." From FourEver Friends, *by Erica Miner*

When I turned thirteen, my father gave me a book with blank pages: my first journal. The pristine pages signified a metaphor for my young life, a symbol of the clean slate with which I was starting my new life as a teenager. In his wisdom, my dad gave me a tool for jumpstarting my eventual career as a writer. What he didn't know was that my teenage journals would someday provide the seeds for a series of novels about four best friends helping each other through the trials of adolescence.

These three precious friendships I formed decades ago blossomed and matured into the closest ones of my life. We met through a mutual love of music, and we all kept music as an essential part of our lives. Most important, the four of us stayed close through our journeys into womanhood. We still support each other in ways we never could have imagined back then.

Friendship is truly a gift, which you will cherish more and more as you grow older. You and your friends help each other grow up. Your friends are a reflection, a mirror of yourself, yet different—a window into other backgrounds, other personalities. You need them and they need you. They help you appreciate your family, the people who loved and nurtured you; yet they give you the strength and courage to go off into a whole new world when the time comes, beyond the comfort zone of home.

It's vital to form and develop these friendships when you are young, for this teaches you how to interact with other friends, companions, colleagues, and loved ones whom you will meet in the future.

I always knew I would be a violinist, though I had no way of knowing I would play in the orchestra of the Metropolitan Opera in New York. But somehow my friends always knew I was destined to become a major player in the musical world.

It was hard work, but they encouraged me, spurred me on to fulfill my potential. Because of their support, I found the confidence to follow my passion, and I encouraged them to pursue theirs. They were always there to support me, even when I left our hometown of Detroit for the land of cultural opportunity, the East Coast. We stayed in touch as best we could through our busy childbearing years. We met each other's children. And when I came back to Detroit to perform with the Met, my friends were there to show their support. That's what friends do: support each other, give each other courage, have fun together. They are, according to mystery writer Edna Buchanan, "the family we choose for ourselves." What would I have done without my friends when I was fourteen or fifteen and despaired of my parents' ever understanding me, or my problems? My three BFF's were both sisters and colleagues. The family I chose for myself.

Now I have put away my violin and taken up writing and speaking as my life's work. I still email these friends, speak with them, and see them whenever possible. As the years pass, they become even more precious to me.

Choose your friends wisely. Then be there for each other. That is a gift that has no price: the gift of a lifetime.

EXERCISE

Journaling Journey

Journaling about your experiences with friendship is a gift you can give yourself. Through journaling you can examine your thoughts, express your joys and fears, and keep track of your journey of self-discovery, both with your friends and on your own. Here's how to get started:

- ★ Create your own special ritual. Find a time of day when you can be quiet and a comfortable place where you can be alone.
- ★ Buy a notebook, a book with blank pages, or anything that will be fun to write in. Invest in a pen that's pretty and comfortable to write with.
- ★ Sit down and let your thoughts and feelings flow. Don't edit your words; just write whatever comes to mind. Talk about what you and your friends did, said and felt that particular day.
- ★ Make the commitment to do this everyday at the same time. Be consistent.

After a while, you will find yourself looking forward to this "alone time." If you feel comfortable about sharing your journal with your friends, you may do so, or you can keep it private, for your own eyes only. When you go back after weeks or months and read your entries, you will learn how your friends are helping you to grow. Appreciate what a gift you are to each other.

☆

"No matter how our paths diverge,
we'll always manage to
come back to our friendship."
Erica Miner

Quote from *FourEver Friends* by Erica Miner
is excerpted with permission of Nightengale Press.

The Gift of GOALS

By Cynthia Brian

Winston Churchill wrote, "It is a mistake to try to look too far ahead. The chain of destiny can only be grasped one link at a time." I believe in the importance of having goals and more importantly of writing them down. When we fail to plan we plan to fail and if we don't know where we are going, we'll never get there.

Every January, people make resolutions to lose weight, earn more money, sleep more hours, travel to distant lands, and spend more time with loved ones. By the beginning of April, most of those great intentions have been long forgotten in the fast paced existence we call life. Although statistics indicate that it only takes thirty days to drop an old habit or learn a new one, most of us just don't stick with our plans long enough to reap any benefits.

Clients of all ages come to me for help in conceiving and achieving their aspirations. Although I have no magic wand, I can offer a few tips that may assist you in setting goals, reaching for the stars, and living your dreams.

★ Focus on the positives in your life instead of the negatives. Make a list of everything *big* and *small* that you accomplished in the last twelve months. Forget about what you did not do. Let it go.

★ Acknowledge your strengths, and pat yourself on the back. Learn to congratulate yourself and celebrate. You'll be astonished at how much you did achieve!

★ Eliminate the excuses from your vocabulary. People say to me that they want to write a book or audition for a movie but "don't have the time, don't know how, don't know if I have the skills, don't think I could do it!" There is only one *now*, so just do it, or quit talking about it.

★ Create a plan of action by breaking down your goals into small, realistic steps. For example, don't say "I am going to lose twenty-five pounds this year," instead say "I will be healthier this year with a goal of losing two pounds per month and I'll weigh 130 pounds by December 1." Those two pounds per month sound doable, while twenty-five pounds feels like a stretch. By the inch it's a cinch.

- ★ Decide how much time you can give to your dreams and stick to it. Again, start small. Allocate one hour a week, or three hours a month or perhaps an uninterrupted weekend. Tackle each obstacle as it arises without letting a monster into your psyche.
- ★ Make a list of everyone who can help you achieve your goals and share your ideas. This is especially important if achieving your dreams impacts the time you spend with friends, family, or co-workers. Don't under estimate the people that love you. Engage them. When you let them know what you are striving for, they are more willing to help you get there. Ask for help from your parents first.
- ★ Get organized. This needs to be in capital letters, so here it is again. GET ORGANIZED. That means organize your workspace, your home life, your backpack, your locker, your closet, your purse, your wallet, your car, and your schedules. If you operate in clutter and chaos, it will be challenging to create anything new in your life.
- ★ Be a list maker. Create a master to-do list. Better yet, create a chart with daily, weekly, and monthly goals. This allows you to see what you have accomplished and what you need to do to get to the next agenda.
- ★ Plan ahead. Interruptions and unexpected emergencies will arise. Allow yourself the space and time you need.
- ★ Be specific. Many teens say they want better grades. But what does "better grades," mean? Do you want to just pass or do you want an "A"? Would receiving a "B" or "C" be acceptable? Other kids have told me they want to be accepted. Again, what does that mean? How do you want to achieve that goal? Will you join a club? Do you want to be part of a social group? Or, are you looking for others to compliment your fashion style? What kind of friend are you looking for? I have often said that my dream home would be on water and I daily envision myself living on a lake. We had a tremendous rainfall, our creeks overflowed and our gardens and driveway flooded. When I looked out in the morning I was living on a rushing river and a lake, but it wasn't exactly what I truly wanted. I wasn't specific enough! Be clear. Be very specific.
- ★ Don't get overwhelmed. Remember to pamper yourself, step back, and re-evaluate your progress as you go along. Your goal is to celebrate the accomplishments, not chide yourself for the setbacks.

- ★ Keep your eye on the prize. Focus on how you will feel when you have reached your dream. It's a process, and to make dreams come true, you have to dream big in the first place.

You will have doubts and you will have down days. No one is 100 percent on track all the time. Work towards your strengths, not your weaknesses. The result will be more balance, more purpose, and most of all, more happiness. People achieve what they think they have the ability to achieve. Hard work, sacrifice, and commitment deserve applause. Create *S.M.A.R.T.* goals and watch your successful habits soar.

By rewarding yourself for your successes and keeping your goals realistic, doable, accountable, and specific, you'll find yourself creating the future you have always wanted.

EXERCISE

S.M.A.R.T. Goals

Goals can be set and accomplished all year long when you make ***S.M.A.R.T.*** goals. ***S.M.A.R.T.*** stands for:

- ★ specific
- ★ measurable
- ★ achieveable
- ★ relevant
- ★ timely

Steps to ***S.M.A.R.T.*** Goals:

- ★ SPECIFIC—learning to speak Chinese is specific while making more money is not. If you want to know if your are designing a smart goal, ask yourself, "What do I mean by that?"
- ★ MEASUREABLE—learning to speak Chinese in thirteen weeks is measurable, while being rich is not. Your actions must be calculable so you know when you have achieved success. Just how much money is *mor*e money-twenty-five cents, one dollar, or two million dollars?

- ★ ACHIEVEABLE—learning to speak Chinese in thirteen weeks so that I can order food in a Chinese restaurant is achievable, while losing fifty pounds in one week is not. Be realistic about what you can truly accomplish. Success breeds success, so set goals that are within reach with self-determination. Don't set yourself up for failure.
- ★ REVELANT—learning to speak Chinese in thirteen weeks so that I can order food in a Chinese restaurant while vacationing in China is relevant. To be relevant, the goal must really matter to you. If you don't have a good reason for doing it, you'll drop the goal after a few weeks of attempts.
- ★ TIMELY—learning to speak Chinese by the time I leave for my vacation to Beijing gives an end point. Even if you want to have a goal forever, put an end date to a cycle, then start anew when accomplished.

The time is now. Work your plan and plan your work. As the sage Yoda said, "Do or do not, there is no try." Stop making useless resolutions. Instead, get out paper and pen to start dreaming. Reach for one small star at a time, and, before long, you'll be playing in a galaxy!

Wishing you a most prosperous, healthy, happy, and thrilling life. Shine, sparkle, and soar.

☆

"You are the star of your own performance.
Create S.M.A.R.T. goals and turn
your passions into profits."
Cynthia Brian

The Gift of
GRATITUDE

By Rena Wilson Fox

As my daughter was nearing the age of thirteen, we decided to move our family overseas for an eighteen-month work assignment. Not only were we leaving her school and friends behind, we were moving to the Middle East. With all the trepidation that comes with moving, our emotional departure was exacerbated by others' fear of that region. My daughter had many goodbyes and tear-filled days before we left.

We arrived at our new home and began our new life. However, with every new experience, my daughter pulled back and became defiant. She was determined to dislike everything. She started school with the attitude that it was something to be survived until she could resume the life she had been living. We encouraged her to try new things like taking guitar lessons or trying out for the badminton team. The options seemed endless, but she couldn't see through the grief she carried and the longing she had for her old life. She locked her heart and closed her mind.

After many heated discussions and my constant encouragement for a positive attitude, I decided I would ask her to email me every day. In her messages, she would tell me three things she was grateful for that day that. At first her list was simple:

"I'm grateful my jeans were clean."

"I'm thankful I have my own bedroom."

"I'm grateful for my family, even though they made me move here..."

As time moved on, her list began to change:

"I'm grateful for blue skies every day!"

"I'm grateful daddy works less here, and we see him more."

"I'm grateful for new friends."

Through the course of her emails, you could see her heart begin to open. She started to allow herself to befriend others without feeling like it was a betrayal of those she left behind. She yearned to dance again and did so without thinking she was somehow cheating on her dance teacher back in Pennsylvania. She started to feel alive again. She began to see the good in the life we had chosen. Her gratitude spilled over, and she was starting to see the privilege of this experience instead of the loss.

She began to look at people and things differently. She began to see *everything* as a gift; from the hot air balloon in the Wadi Rum desert, to sea glass in the Red Sea, to floating effortlessly in the Dead Sea. Then she began to recognize gratitude in others as well, especially those with very few material possessions. She could sense the joy people had when they were truly open and grateful for their lives. The gratitude habit changed her from the inside out.

This change allowed her to meet wonderful friends that are certain to be life long, and she cried as hard leaving eighteen months later as she had when she arrived. Her heart was fully opened. She had learned that there is always something to be grateful for every day, even through the most difficult of times.

EXERCISE

Great Grateful

Start a journal or notebook, writing down things you are grateful for at the end of every day. List at least three things. If it seems difficult to come up with things at first, write whatever you can think of, even if it seems insignificant or silly. As time goes on, you will start looking at a sunrise or beautiful flower, knowing it will be on your list at the end of the day! Even on your worst days, think of three things and remember that when you look at things with gratitude in your heart, joy will return.

☆

"Real gratitude creates joy!"
Rena Wilson Fox

The Gift of GREEN

By Cynthia Brian

Do you remember Kermit, the Frog moaning about the difficulty of being green? He really liked being green, except he thought he blended into the landscape too much to be noticed. The lyrics to Kermit's song are about accepting and prizing our uniqueness rather than feeling estranged and inferior because we are different and longing to be like the perceived majority. Although his song was not written about the environment, I think that the modern-day Kermit would be proud to be green in color as well as ecologically prudent. We all need to honor the greening of the world.

It seems that everyone is talking or writing about being eco-friendly, environmentally correct, recycling, or green washing. How can we be better stewards of our earth?

We live in a disposable society with more garbage in our dumps than ever before. Whether global warming is a natural cycle or a forerunner of disaster, living with the rhythm of Mother Nature influences us more than we know. Any time is a great time to start living consciously, and when we are young is the best time of all.

When I was growing up on the farm, we recycled and reused everything. I sewed my own clothes, grew my own vegetables, and refinished furniture that was in the barn. In those days it was called being frugal, but today frugal is fabulous. My siblings and I always made gifts from scraps of other things. One year for Christmas we made our Godmothers Santa pillows. Each holiday, our Godmothers would proudly display our creations, often taking their naps on our comfortable cushions. This year, Aunt Helen's Santa pillow ripped, and she brought it to my sister Debbie, laughing hysterically. "Deb, all these years I've slept on this great pillow, and, when it ripped, I finally saw the stuffing inside," she giggled. Debbie grabbed the pillow and pulled out the contents—various under garments, nylons, rags, blouses, and other cast offs from four decades ago. Now, that was being clean green!

When I lived in Holland as a teenager, I never saw a paper bag, paper plate, or paper napkin. Each person in the house was given a linen napkin with a napkin ring. At every meal, we all took our individual napkins from their rings and reused the cloth napkins. When the napkin was soiled, it was washed. We ate on sturdy china plates with flatware—no plastic or paper. We went to the store carrying mesh bags and bought only enough food to fit into the bags we could carry. There was no waste.

As a result of our second-hand recycling expertise and experiencing how people in other lands lived, I feel satisfied that over the years I have done my part to enable our planet to survive. Yet there is always more I can do. Here are a few ways you can be more environmentally savvy and help reduce your carbon footprint.

★ Buy products with no packaging or packaging that you can repurpose.

★ Buy a canvas tote and use it for all your shopping instead of getting plastic or paper bags from the store. (For inexpensive custom created canvas bags, visit www.karmonykollection.com or www.myspace.com/karmonyklutches)

★ Don't use paper napkins, paper towels, or paper plates. It is less expensive and less wasteful to wash your napkins, towels, and plates.

★ Instead of tossing out empty plastic water bottles, use a refillable bottle.

★ Bring your lunch to school or work in reusable boxes.

★ Collect rain water to water your outdoor plants and shower water to water your indoor greenery.

★ Turn off the lights when you leave a room, and power down your computer.

★ Ask your parents to buy only green cleaning products.

★ Use public transportation, walk, or bike.

★ Skip the elevator and use the stairs.

★ Borrow books from the library or buy your books from the charity, Be the Star You Are!, which rescues new, soon-to-be destroyed tomes. (www.bethestaryouare.org)

★ Donate your teen magazines to shelters, or share with your friends.

★ Pick up trash, and do not litter—ever!

★ Learn to sew, paint, reupholster, re-finish, and other skills that will help you reuse hand-me-downs.

★ Grow live plants in your room to clean your air.

★ Don't smoke—it pollutes the air, your friends, and your lungs.

★ Participate in beach or park clean-up days.

★ Talk a walk on your local trails to learn about flora and fauna in your area.

★ Plant an herb and vegetable garden to use in the kitchen.

- ★ Learn to compost. Check for free composting classes in your neighborhood.
- ★ Set up a worm bin to enrich your garden's soil. It's fun!
- ★ *Eat locally grown organic vegetables, eggs, and fruits.
- ★ Give your outgrown clothing to Goodwill or an organization that can use it.
- ★ Turn down the heat, and wear a warmer sweater when you are cold.
- ★ Dispose of waste appropriately, and buy only earth-friendly products.
- ★ Volunteer your time to a charity that believes in saving the planet.

Each person can make a difference. Turn your trash into treasures by sharing your castoffs with those less fortunate. Every step you take to be green helps. The habits you acquire now will serve you and the planet well for the rest of you life. Become more like Kermit, the Frog. Be unique. Be different. Be tolerant. Be your best self. But also be happy blending in and being green.

EXERCISE

Living Green

Have a family meeting to decide ways that you can save energy and become green. Brainstorm together, write down your ideas, and initiate a reward system on a monthly basis for each person who abides by the new set of living green tools. Green living is more attainable and easier than you may think, and it will probably save your family money too. Reduce, reclaim, reuse, recycle, remake, reenergize, reinvent, re-do, refurbish. Go green today…the third star from the sun requires your participation to survive.

☆

"It's easy being green
because green is what I want to be!"
Cynthia Brian

The Gift of
HAPPINESS

By M.J. Ryan

I wanted to thank someone who had been kind to me. So I sent a bouquet of roses to her office. When ordering, I found out that peach symbolize appreciation, so I delighted in sending an extra, nonverbal message. I imagined what a surprise they would be, which pleased me even more.

I first started to enjoy the happiness that comes from giving to others when my friends and I published the book *Random Acts of Kindness.* Suddenly I was flooded with letters (this was in the dinosaur days before email) from people telling me about the joy they'd experienced as doers of these acts. I will never forget the letter from the high school senior who told me that he'd been going to kill himself until he read the book and decided that life was worth living. He inspired me to become more kind to strangers as well as to those I'm close to. Like the boy who didn't kill himself, I got happier.

The reason we feel happy when we spread happiness is because we experience something I've never heard spoken of in Western culture. I've just finished reading over fifty books on happiness and only one mentions it. Buddhists call it *mudita*—sympathetic joy. It's an upwelling of the heart at the happiness of someone else.

Sympathetic joy is the opposite of envy. It's one of the reasons why giving, when it comes from a genuine feeling of overflow-wanting to bring happiness to someone else rather than from a sense that we have to-feels so good. We experience in ourselves the good feelings of the other person.

Actually the giver gets a double whammy of happiness—anticipatory joy in thinking of how the person is going to feel, as well as the actual moment when he or she receives the gift. Sympathetic joy is such a wonderful feeling that you don't even have to be there when the person receives the gift to feel great. That's what's behind random acts of kindness. For instance, just thinking about how the person is going to feel when you put a quarter in the parking meter and he doesn't get a ticket gives you a jolt of pleasure.

You don't have to buy elaborate gifts or spend a lot of time or effort. You can get the boost from giving to others in many ways: surprises to a relative in the form of a text message, the perfect card for a friend.

Have you ever offered thanks for a courtesy to someone who replied, "My pleasure"? It truly is a pleasure to spread kindness, even if it's simply holding the door for someone who is struggling with a load of packages.

EXERCISE

Practicing Acts of Happiness

Commit to giving something, no matter how small, every day for a week. In the Jewish tradition a *mitzvah,* literally a blessing, is an act of kindness, preferably anonymous for which no acknowledgment or reward is expected. A kind word, a smile to someone you know is going through tough times, an offer to help your sibling, an email out of the blue thanking someone for the impact he's had on your life. Even if you don't feel great, do it anyway for a week and notice what effect it has. Do you feel more joyful, more connected to others, and happy to be alive? Make someone else happy! Have you done your *mitzvah* for the day?

☆

"Happiness is a perfume which you cannot pour on others without getting a few drops on yourself."
Louis L. Mann

The Gift of
HEALING

By Arlyn Van Dyke

The day was bitterly cold. A bone-chilling blizzard had passed through the Iowa countryside as I was on my way home with a pheasant in hand when a snowdrift stopped the tractor that I was riding. In between thinking of the dinner we were going to enjoy and the tractor being stuck in the snow, all hell broke loose. To my left I heard an ear numbing sound, my left arm jerked upwards and then something heavy hit my head. My twenty-gauge shotgun had automatically discharged taking most of my left arm with it. The blood that was draining from the left sleeve of my winter jacket sounded like water running from the garden hose. I knew I was in trouble.

I could see the farmyard but no one was within range that could help me. With my arm dangling at my side, I squeezed the bloody jacket sleeve, hoping to halt the bleeding. I started walking toward our farm where I knew my dad would be working with the animals. As my legs weakened, I saw my dad exit the barn. "Help me dad, " I weakly uttered.

Dad drove the car as fast as a NASCAR driver over the gravel road between our farm and the local hospital. While I lay on the doctor's examining table, I remember the doctor cutting my sleeve off as parts of my arm fell onto the table. Shotgun shell BB's bounced around the room. The prognosis wasn't good.

The doctor gravely announced, "Son, that arm has to come off immediately." The pain was excruciating as I attempted to move my thumb and index finger. I looked first into the eyes of the doctor, then into those of my dad, then back again to the physician. "Amputation is not an option," I responded weakly. The doctor looked at my dad as if to say you better talk to this young man. This time gazing directly at my pop, I repeated, "amputation is not an option." With all the courage that a fourteen-year-old could muster, I asked the doctor if he knew of anyone who could save my arm. He said he would make a few calls on my behalf. After what seemed an eternity, the doctor returned to the examination room. He had found a surgeon who practiced seventy-five miles away who agreed to help as long as we moved quickly. Immediately, my dad volunteered to drive me, but the doctor said that going by local emergency ambulance would get me there sooner. Although I was suffering the worst pain I had ever experienced, I refused the pain medication offered, because I wanted to be lucid when I spoke to the surgeon.

I vividly remember every bump on that highway to Sioux City, Iowa. As much as I wanted the ambulance driver to slow down to ease the trauma, I also knew speed was the key to my survival. I clenched my teeth and endured.

Suddenly, I felt someone grab my left arm. Again, I was stretched out on an examining table. The surgeon had wire-rim glasses, strawberry-blonde hair, blond eyelashes, warm hands, and a calming demeanor. "I have been waiting for you. I am Dr. Graham," he calmly and caringly stated. He went on to tell me that the wound was filled with debris from the layers of clothing that I had been wearing. Infection was going to be my greatest enemy. "I understand that you think this arm can be saved," Dr. Graham smiled. I remember looking at his face and telling him that if he could clean it up, I would take care of rest. He placed his warm hand gently on my shoulder and patted his understanding. "Well, I have some work to do now," he said quietly. "Do you need anything for that pain?" "Yes, *please*," is all I remember whispering before I lost consciousness.

When I awoke the next day, my mom was sitting at my bedside looking both worried and sad. I asked her if I still had my arm. She smiled. "You sure do, son." I had taken a full load from that twenty gauge shotgun point-blank on the inside of my left elbow. The gun blast removed the inside half of my elbow, two inches of the humerus and fractured my radius and ulnar bones. The ulnar nerve was severed, and two of my fingers did not move. The blast from the gun had removed most of my biceps muscle, but spared all of my major arteries. After my arm went through stages of color changes and multiple injections of antibiotics, I was able to leave the hospital one month later.

My life had changed, the way I looked changed. I knew that I looked different to my friends. And I was determined to heal myself and to help heal others.

My world has metamorphosed since that cold January afternoon. That caring gentleman with wire rim glasses became my physician, inspiration, and mentor. Dr. Graham not only saved my arm, he saved my life with his empathy, understanding, and healing. He even went a step further—he provided the encouragement and finances for me to go to college where I earned a Bachelor of Science with a major in science and pre-physical therapy followed by a degree in physical therapy from the University of Iowa. Today, I am a physical therapist and I gratefully remember Dr. Graham whenever I touch my patients and assure them that they too will be okay.

EXERCISE

Prescription for Healing

Bad things happen even when we are good. Look for the miracles and opportunities for healing your heart, soul, and body in any dire situation. Each one of us harbors a doctor within. Heal thyself!

☆

"There are no mistakes. The events we bring upon ourselves, no matter how unpleasant, are necessary to learn what we need to learn; whatever steps we take, they're necessary to reach the places we've chosen to go."
Richard Bach

The Gift of HOPE

By C. Hope Clark

My parents expected me to perform my best as a child, which usually meant honor roll and near perfection. My IQ scored high, and teachers treated me differently, almost reverently. I amassed awards in school, wondering what career path I was expected to pursue…what path would please my parents and teachers the most.

I chose an agricultural major in college. Nature soothed me, and the science of soils and plants intrigued my intellect. My agriculture degree carried me into the federal government. I landed the job easily, my academic achievement speaking on my behalf. As a quick study, I learned fast, and soon farmers and rural residents came to me for advice in financial matters. Number crunching felt great. But helping people felt phenomenal. A spark flickered deep inside me; flashing bright each time I kept farmers on their farms or families in their homes.

My eager effort to aid people came to the attention of my employer. Soon I became a troubleshooter, noted for solving huge financial dilemmas for clients in a crisis. Promotions came fast. I moved up into a managerial position. But my spark dimmed as my career path removed me from directly assisting others.

Seeking Solace, I returned to writing, a love I held in high school and college. I wrote under my middle name instead of my first, to keep my writing life separate from my daytime career. I loved the alter ego. My ability to string words together released the stresses of the day. I came home from the office and wrote in the dark shadows of my bedroom after everyone slept, pecking the keyboard until my eyelids fell shut. Surprisingly, I caught myself wondering about the mission of my life again, writing about my internal struggle to find purpose, returning to those feelings held as a teenager.

One weekend, an editor and I conversed about an assignment, but the topic shifted to her financial problems. I advised her as I'd once done with my rural customers. Thrilled, she told her friends. My email box began filling with similar requests. I loved helping people, but the extensive emails took me away from my writing. After all, I wanted to write a great novel, not play Dear Abby.

But the emails increased. I established a newsletter so I didn't have to answer so many emails. I taught myself html and created a web site. In a few months, I had a thousand followers. In a year, two thousand. The more I tried to write for myself, the bigger the web site and newsletters grew. People loved my guidance, my voice, and my support for their dream to write. My own writing exploded, improving in leaps and bounds, becoming more colorful and exciting with each editorial, each article, and each feature piece that aided other writers.

Then one night as I pounded away at an upbeat essay, it hit me. The spark had stealthily slipped back into my life, blazing with stimulation. Dumbfounded, I sat back in my chair. I recognized this old heart-pounding feeling of satisfaction. What did my newsletter for struggling writers have in common with farmers and poor rural residents?

Hope. I offered hope.

It wasn't about the awards and accomplishments I could earn for me. My purpose was to enable and empower others. The more help I gave away, the more I thrived. My purpose was spotlighting hope, defining second chances, lighting the path to options to make other lives better.

I softly laughed. My middle name, my writing name, is Hope.

EXERCISE

Finding Hope

Think of all the people in your life, past and present. Who excited you? Who gave you hope to seek goals and improve yourself? What characteristics of this person captured your attention and helped you find the right path to a better you?

Think of friends who need hope. Can you inspire them? Can you make them feel better about themselves and improve their lives?

Try to keep your eyes open and identify those who could use a ray of your hope. Then write about the experience in your journal so you can refer back to it months later. You'll empower yourself both when you record the event and later when you recall the moment.

☆

"Hope for the good in others, and you'll find it in yourself."
C. Hope Clark

The Gift of HUMOR

By Dr. Joel Goodman

Dr. Jim Boren wanted to prevent World War III.

His strategy was based on the notion that "laughter" has no accent." This became the theme for Jim's comedic cultural connection between the United States and what was then the Soviet Union. In the midst of the not-so-funny Cold War, Jim thought we should use humor to build bridges between our two countries and cultures.

I had the good fortune to be one of five Americans who traveled to Moscow for a three-week joyous jaunt to start this exchange program. When I told friends about this trip, they were incredulous and wondered aloud, "Do Russians have a sense of humor?" What tickled me was that when we arrived in Moscow, one of the first questions from the Soviets was, "Do Americans have a sense of humor?"

I am happy to report the mutual, mirthful, meaningful discovery that a sense of humor is a quality that we shared. We all realized that we had a lot more in common as "humor beings" than our differences.

I was delighted that this comedic cultural exchange continued on our side of the ocean. A group of five top Soviet humorists made their first stop in the U.S. at the home of The Humor Project in Saratoga Springs, New York. We arranged a variety of events for the Soviets—a public forum attended by hundreds of people in our community, a visit to an elementary school, and a trip to a local hospital at which we had set up a humor room to help lift the (comic) spirits of patients.

We were especially excited about a peak experience that we had planned for our visitors as a surprise: a hot air balloon festival at the height of the glorious fall foliage in the Adirondack Mountains. Each of five balloons carried one American, one Soviet, and the balloonist. I was in the balloon with Andrey Benyukh, an English-speaking, a frizzy-haired and mustachioed editor at *Krokodil* (the national Soviet humor magazine).

As we ascended above the breathtaking grandeur of Lake George, I realized that Andrey was out of breath for another reason. In a trembling voice, he confessed with a shiver, "I am deathly afraid of heights!"

This was not a great discovery for me to make at two thousand feet above the color-splashed mountains. In the snug space of our balloon basket, Andrey was holding on to me for dear life. It was during this time aloft that we began kidding around, even though we did not have a translator aboard. We moved from "grim and bear it" to "grin and share it." Before long, Andrey's trembling with fear morphed into shaking with laughter. Our guess-you-had-to-be-there banter ranged from spontaneous satire ("Being in this balloon, it's clear that politicians aren't the only ones filled with hot air!") to playing with the situation ("Being in a hot air balloon with a fear of heights... is the height of silliness!").

In the midst of our comedic camaraderie, I also learned that Andrey's daughter's name is Alica. I told him that my daughter is Alyssa. In that moment, we both knew in our hearts that we were doing this humor exchange program to provide a safe, loving, laughing legacy for our children. The hot air balloon became the metaphor-that we were in this world together (literally and figuratively), and that we would either crash or rise to the occasion together.

In the cozy confines of the hot air balloon basket, I appreciated again that levity defies gravity...and that laughter has no accent. I was also reminded of Erma Bombeck's wonderful wit and wisdom: "When humor goes, there goes civilization!" My up-close-and-personal experience with Andrey reinforced the idea that "Laughter is the shortest distance between two people...and between two peoples."

EXERCISE

Habit of Farce

Lots of people have *homework* assignments. For the next twenty-one days enjoy any or all of the following *homeplay* assignments.

- ★ Call a mental "timeout" for five minutes each day to look for the humor in the world around you (and within you).
- ★ Keep a humor diary of your comic visions.
- ★ The next time you are in a stressful situation, ask yourself how your favorite comedian would see this circumstance. This can be a great way for you to reframe and to transform stress into laughter.
- ★ Think of a friend or family member who could use a humor boost. Give that person the gift of laughter by sharing a joke or cartoon that would tickle his or her funny bone.

In the process of performing these *homeplay* exercises, you will also discover that laughter is the shortest distance between two people. The language of humor has no boundaries.

☆

"Seven days without laughter...
make one weak."
Joel Goodman

The Gift of IMAGINATION

By Cynthia Brian

The sun was shining brightly, and the jonquils were blooming that January winter day so many years ago when my brothers, sisters, and I awoke to find strands of gleaming jewelry strung everywhere on the bushes and grape vines around the house. Barefoot, we ran outside, not believing our eyes. They had come. The Kings had arrived.

The holiday was "Twelfth Night" or "Three Wise Kings Day," celebrated on January 6, which is exactly twelve days after Christmas. The celebration was created to honor the Magi who followed the Star of Bethlehem to visit Baby Jesus over two thousand years ago. Because we are Swiss-Italian and lived in the country, mom and dad always told us it was easier for the Three Wise Kings to park their camels outside our house than a house in the city. We had no reason not to believe them.

We loved Three Wise Kings Day because the Magi made us feel special. No one else in our school seemed to receive a nightfall visitation from these Middle Eastern monarchs. And though legend proclaims that the Three Kings brought Jesus gold, frankincense, and myrrh, we were very pleased to receive a piece of fruit, a bit of candy, and about twenty-five cents in coins from them each year.

But this year was different. They had actually brought us jewels and riches beyond our wildest dreams. I vividly remember the sensation of utter delight when we spotted the shimmering trinkets hanging from the trees! I will never forget the utter thrill of knowing that our landscape was adorned with valuable ornaments from a land far, far away.

"We're rich, we're rich!" my siblings shouted. Although we loved the fruit the Magi left us, seeing the glimmering baubles adorning our very own vines was quite magnificent. To furthering the illusion, we found camels' hoof prints and a good amount of camel dung scattered throughout the garden. To top it all off, a note was attached to one of the bushes, an announcement that it had been a great year for the Magi, so they had decided to share their wealth with us.

We couldn't wait to go to school to tell our teachers and all our friends about these extraordinary gifts. Surely others had experienced their delights. But no one else had.

In fact, our ingenious parents had created the illusion solely for us with used costume jewelry from a thrift shop and horse manure from our very own barn. My dad had brought out the horses to make the hoof prints, but naturally, we just *knew* they were camel prints. The nuns at school recall our wide-eyed awe when we retold the tale, and they chose to keep our parents' secret. When we told the other children, we were met with disappointed looks. To our dismay, none of them had encountered such riches on the branches of their trees. We immediately shared our booty.

Had we inspected the coins and jewels carefully, we would have easily seen that they were old, broken, rusted, and used. But our imaginations took hold, helping us to visualize the long, dusty trek from the Holy Land to our garden. Our parents' imagination has offered us years of enjoyable memories.

When we allow that creative part of our mind to wander, magic happens. We aren't stuck in the mud of reality, and we actually can envision a new truth. It has been said that necessity is the mother of invention. I think that imagination inspires ingenuity. Don't play it safe in life. Allow yourself the time to dream, to look up at the stars, and to believe in the unbelievable. We are never too old to invent a playful approach to living.

EXERCISE

Imagine

Lie down on the grass in your backyard or in a park. Look up at the clouds. If it's winter and you can't go outside, lie on your bed, look at the shadows and cracks on the ceiling. What do you see? Horses racing? Monsters roaring? Dancing cows? Use your imagination to paint pictures in your mind of what the vapors or shapes are displaying. Now shut your eyes and dream of something that you really want and need. See it in your mind, and then experience it with all your senses. Then open your eyes, stare at the heavens, and find what you are looking for. Imagine your reality and you can attain it.

☆

"There are no limitations to the mind except those we acknowledge; both poverty and riches are the offspring of thought."
Napoleon Hill

The Gift of
IMPROVISATION

By Cynthia Brian

Life is filled with twists and turns as every one of us soon learns. When you don't know exactly what to do, knowing how to improvise is indeed a welcome gift.

Campus life at U.C.L.A. was thrilling for any teenager, but especially for someone like me who was raised in the country. Throughout high school I had been active in numerous clubs and extracurricular sports and had looked forward to participating in college activities. U.C.L.A. offered a plethora of mind-boggling opportunities and choices. Since I was now living in Southern California, not far from the beautiful warm beaches, I decided to learn to scuba dive. Twice a week I took intensive underwater courses. It was exhilarating when I received my N.A.U.I. certification on a dive in the open ocean. From the moment I experienced the beauty under the sea, I was hooked.

U.C.L.A. boasted a thriving scuba club headed by the then President of the National Association of Underwater Instructors; aka N.A.U.I. Having our leader so deeply involved with N.A.U.I. was a benefit. We willingly volunteered as guinea pigs, testing numerous underwater devices from scooters to helmets. Every weekend a boat dive was organized to the Channel Islands where we would buddy up to take the plunge amid the kelp fields and rock formations. Some weeks we'd dive for abalone; others we'd harvest scallops to eat raw on the boat.

The most memorable trip, however, was the lobster hunt.

Our club carpooled to Santa Barbara one Friday evening where we settled into sleeping bags on the dive boat. Before dawn, the captain set out on a turbulent sea to navigate to the islands. Our small boat was rocking and rolling as the wind pummeled the craft. Feeling a bit woozy, I went to use the outdoor toilet and got locked inside. "Please don't let this boat sink, " I prayed as I pounded on the door, hoping someone would hear me. Alas, the roar of the engine masked my screams for help. Not wanting to be found at the bottom of the ocean drowned in a locked bathroom I had to improvise an escape. My hairclip became the tool I used to spring the lock. In the blackness, I tiptoed back to my bunk where my fellow divers slept soundly oblivious to my alarming plight and adept escape.

By the time we arrived at our dive location, the seas had calmed, the sun was shining, and I had forgotten about my frightening bathroom experience. We were each provided with a mesh bag and given instructions on how to corral a lobster. After two dives, I had captured four big "bugs", a diver's pet name for lobsters, the smallest weighing twelve pounds. The dive was successful for everyone. The crustaceans were marked and put in a gargantuan salt-water tank.

It was past midnight when I indulged in a hot shower at my apartment before seeking a place to keep my lobsters for the night. The door to my roommate's bedroom was closed, indicating she was sound asleep. Not having an aquarium large enough, I improvised by filling the bathtub with cold water and sea salt. My four gigantic lobsters were provided with a makeshift habitat until morning when they'd be brought to the kitchen for preparation. I climbed into my warm bed, dreaming about the smiling faces of my college friends drooling over the forthcoming feast.

The blood curdling screams startled me awake about an hour later. I ran from my room to see my panic stricken friend shrieking and yelling about monster spiders in the bathroom. My heart stopped! Janet had not been snugly asleep as I thought, but instead had been out on date. Not wanting to wake me when she entered, she had turned on the water in the shower tub in the dark, got undressed, and stepped in. Instantly, the sea creatures attacked!

It took some time to calm her nerves while I provided an explanation. All was forgiven the following day when we invited the students in our small apartment complex for a lobster feast.

Boy and Girl Scouts learn to be prepared. Actors learn to ad-lib. Everyone needs to know how to manage in unfamiliar circumstances. At one time or another, we will all face a strange situation where we have no prior experience. This is where we make it up as we go. Just as I used the hairclip to free me from the head jail, and the bathtub to keep my sea creatures alive, Janet coped with clawed visitors in her tub. Fortunately for me, we are still friends, and throughout the years we have laughed at my outrageous improvisational act, although she makes sure to turn on the light whenever she bathes at my home!

EXERCISE

Robinson Crusoe to the Rescue

If you were stranded on a desert island with only one other person, who would that person be and how would you survive? How would you build shelter? Where would you get food and water? What would you do for entertainment? Daniel DeFoe's novel published in 1719 was based on a real life cast away, Alexander Selkirk , who improvised for four years on a remote Pacific Island. For an entertaining and informative read, pick up a copy of *The Life and Adventures of Robinson Crusoe.* You may never get lost at sea, trapped in a toilet, or discover sea spiders in your bathtub, but you will experience circumstances when knowing the skill of improvisation will save the day!

☆

"When you don't know what to say
or do, be wise and improvise!"
Cynthia Brian

The Gift of INDIVIDUALITY

By Cynthia Brian

When I was a student at the University of Bordeaux in France, I was constantly asked if I was a relative of Sophia Loren. Being one hundred percent Italian, I was thrilled with this observation interpreted as a compliment. After returning to California, I attended CAL Berkeley while working for the airlines for the travel perks. On the streets of San Francisco, total strangers would come up to ask for my autograph. Surprised and hesitant, I signed my name. In those days, I didn't have a television set so it wasn't until months later when I was booking innumerable modeling assignments that I understood the brouhaha. My agent explained that a new TV program called *Charlie's Angels* debuted a new super star, Farrah Fawcett, and, luckily for my agency, I looked just like her!

At first I hated being mistaken for someone else. I was my own person, and I was determined to make it on my own merits. As much as I admired Sophia, I didn't want to copy her. And who was this new celebrity interloper, Farrah, stealing my individuality? During this time, my agency changed my Italian surname to "Brian" because it was more Anglo-Saxon. They were convinced that either their clients were prejudiced against Italians or that my blue-eyed blond self was not the stereotypical Italian expected on the set.

For *Cynthia Brian* jobs came quickly and easily. I modeled consistently, then branched into TV and films. I earned enough money to allow me to quit the airlines job. However, it soon became apparent that my #1 asset was my resemblance to Farrah Fawcett. When a buyer couldn't afford the high fees Farrah was earning, my agent was willing to negotiate a reasonable deal. The first time I was Farrah's stunt double on a film, our similarity was truly disconcerting for both of us. When my own mother couldn't tell us apart, I knew I was in trouble. "I saw you on TV last night, Cynthia, and you really need to wear different clothes. Those were way too revealing, and your voice was so high," admonished my mother. Of course it was Farrah she witnessed, not me.

Resembling an established star too closely can sabotage a career. An old Chinese proverb advises, "You can't push the river. You have to let it flow." I took the advice to heart, and quit worrying about looking so much like Farrah. "Que sera, sera" became my motto. Being *Farrah* was magical and frightening, teaching me lessons that have served me well since I came into my own. There were and are still plenty of jobs for the unique individual named *Cynthia Brian*.

Marching to the tune of your own drum is a habit I recommend. Individuality is more important than imitation. Enjoy a real life. Being on TV, in commercials, films, and billboards is fun, but can also create emptiness. Make sure your days are filled with other interests, friends, family, animals, and love. Sitting by the phone is a lousy playground. If your work resembles someone else's—be it a performer, scientist, writer, painter, musician, or whatever—learn from it, but never give up your individual talent just because someone else is already pursuing your area of interest. Expand your area of expertise, tap into your gifts, and do your own thing. Research shows that people do not become high performers by imitating others, but by being themselves. High performance occurs when a person goes beyond their own expectations in ways that are unique to them, consistently and repeatedly. In other words, state your plan, then exceed it in every way. Proclaim your vision and your mission. Claim your identity.

Here are a few tips that helped me own my individual personality. I believe they'll aid you as well in all your endeavors.

- ★ Be positive, optimistic, and think big. If you feel you are worthless, so will everyone else. Love thyself first, and foremost.
- ★ Be prepared, patient, prudent, and persevering. If you want to predict the future, you must create it yourself. Never give up.
- ★ Ask for help. Finding a reputable coach, or consultant that you trust is essential to help you navigate the murky waters of any business. If you choose the performing arts, know that agents and managers come and go. Enticing scams are everywhere. If it sounds too good to be true, it is, plain and simple. Find yourself a mentor.
- ★ Be real. It's *great* to portray someone else. (In fact, that's what acting is all about.) Just don't lose yourself in pretending.
- ★ Seize the day. Be professional, pound the pavement, network, connect, and be your own advocate. Only you can make *you* a success.

My days of being *Farrah* are long gone. We no longer look similar, yet I'm grateful to her for sharing her stardom with me and hope her life is as blessed and fulfilled as mine. Today I am called *The Oprah of the Airwaves,* not because of my resemblance to the TV queen, but because of my interviewing skills on the radio. I no longer fight such comparisons because I am comfortable in my own skin and with my individual talents. My husband would be delighted if I were to age to look like Sophia because she is his all time favorite female. Today when people ask me for my autograph, they expect to see *Cynthia Brian* scrawled on their book jacket. And I chuckle when I'm told, "You know who used to look like you? Farrah Fawcett!"

EXERCISE

Who are You?

A television game show debuted in the 1950's called *What's My Line?* Celebrity panelists would try to guess the occupation of the contestants. The more individualistic the contestant, the more difficult it was to guess what they did.

If you were a contestant on a modern teen version of *What's My Line?*, would the panelists be able to guess your passions and strengths? Are you the person they think you are? Are you expressing your individuality, or are you a copycat? Find out what's underneath your exterior and celebrate the distinctive personage called *you*. There has never been nor will ever be anyone with your exact combinations of strengths, weaknesses, talents, skills, and foibles. Celebrate your individuality!

☆

"Be yourself, your only self,
your greatest self.
You already are a star!"
Cynthia Brian

The Gift of KINDNESS

By Cynthia Brian

Kindness is a gentle, powerful act. It is the quality of being pleasant, friendly, and concerned for others. Being kind is a way to make daily life better for yourself as well as others. Kindness can change a bad day into a great day for everyone. Kindness helps people feel good about themselves and others.

I read once that a man has to live with himself and see to it that he always has good company. As adolescents, we really attempt to fit in, and sometimes we trust those who are not kind, nor amiable companions.

Kristen was an exceptional athlete, with a quick laugh and kind word for everybody. Her family was athletic, and together they spent weekends water skiing, snow skiing, and bicycling. In her first year of college, Kristen was drafted to the water ski team where, although she was a young freshman, she garnered first place in the championships. After her first win, she slept in the communal room with her female squad, content in the knowledge that she had done her part to bring victory to new team. She awoke in the morning to find her long blond locks severed and scattered on the floor. The reigning champ felt usurped and had taken her revenge by cutting Kristen's hair. A similar act of jealousy had been my experience as well in high school. Despite the attacks, we continued to be kind.

Jealousy and envy are poison to the soul of humanity. There is only room for great kindness and compassion. These harrowing experiences taught both Kristen and I to be kind instead of competitive. We may not remember what people say to us in life. We will remember what they did to us and how they made us feel. Kindness is a virtue that manifests from our deepest being. It is who we are and what we become.

A random act of kindness was bestowed on my best girlfriend, Eileen and I. We were on the Education Abroad Program from U.C.L.A., going to the Université de Bordeaux in France. During a February school holiday, we trekked to the south of France to participate in the lavish French Mardi Gras, called *Carnival.* The first day we were both robbed. We were hundreds of miles from our apartments in Bordeaux and thousands of miles from California without a franc between us. Since the American Embassy and American Express offices were closed for the holiday, we were stuck. Fortunately, the hotel manager was kind enough to allow us to stay in the hotel until we could acquire cash. However we had no money for food. Our only nourishment was the café au lait, de pain, de beurre, et de comfiture (coffee with milk, bread, butter, and jam) that was served in the breakfast room in the morning. After two days of watching us dip sugar cubes in our mugs and slowly savor the flavor, a lady at another table asked us why we were not eating. We told her our story of being robbed, and she immediately ordered meals for us. Then she went a step further, digging into her handbag and pressing enough francs into our hands to get us back to school in Bordeaux. Although we were grateful, we attempted to refuse her kind offer. "No, you take this" she insisted. "If my daughters were stranded in a foreign city, I hope that a stranger would help them get home. It's my gift." We did make it back to Bordeaux and immediately sent her repayment with our gratitude. Neither Eileen nor I will ever forget the simple kindness of this total stranger.

One of my favorite poets as a teenager was Kahil Gibran. His writings touched me deeply. "Tenderness and kindness are not signs of weakness and despair, but manifestations of strength and resolutions," he wrote. I have always found that the kinder and more thoughtful a person is, the easier it is to find kindness in others. Look for the good in others and allow their light to shine.

Be gentle. Be loving. Be considerate. Be humane. Be compassionate. Be thoughtful. Be kind.

EXERCISE

Random Acts of Kindness

Your assignment today is to find as many quotes as you can that emphasize kindness and enter them in your journal. Implement kindness in your daily deeds without expectation of return. Here are my favorite adages and authors of kind words.

★ Let no one ever come to you without leaving better and happier. Be the living expression of God's kindness: kindness in your face, kindness in your eyes, kindness in your smile. *Mother Teresa*

★ Beginning today, treat everyone you meet as if they were going to be dead by midnight. Extend to them all the care, kindness, and understanding you can muster, and do it with no thought of any reward. Your life will never be the same again. *Og Mandino*

★ I expect to pass through this world but once. Any good, therefore, that I can do, or any kindness that I can show to any fellow creature, let me do it now. Let me not defer or neglect it, for I shall not pass this way again. *William Penn*

★ The kinder and more thoughtful a person is, the more kindness they can find in other people. *Leo Tolstoy*

★ If you want to win friends, make it a point to remember them. If you remember my name, you pay me a subtle compliment; you indicate that I have made an impression on you. Remember my name and you add to my feeling of importance. *Dale Carnegie*

★ May I never get too busy in my own affairs that I fail to respond to the needs of others with kindness and compassion. *Thomas Jefferson*

Ask yourself what you can do to be kind today. Make someone smile. As my mother always taught us, "You'll catch more bees with honey than with vinegar!" You have the power to spread benevolence, joy, and goodwill. Create peace on the planet through kindness and empathy. Do you dare to care?

☆

"You become kind by being kind.
Kindness is a gift to yourself."
Cynthia Brian

The Gift of LAUGHTER

By Jill Byington

In the early days of the Internet, I joined a female discussion forum. Soon I was conversing with women from all over the world, some of whom included initials in the place of entire phrases. The most popular were "lol" and "roflol" which, as I soon found out, mean "laughing out loud" and "rolling on the floor laughing out loud." I also learned that certain punctuation looked at sideways can replace a smile. :-)

Those on the forum who didn't use these simple techniques to communicate laughter or a smile were often misunderstood, leading to meaningless arguments and hurt feelings. Laughter, I concluded, is so important to us as human beings that when we invent a new way to communicate we also must invent a new way to laugh and smile. In fact, laughter is so imbedded in us that even infants who are deaf and blind laugh.

Consider just the following few benefits of laughter:

Laughter can help you learn. Some time in the early 1920s, when there were only forty-eight United States, my Grandpa George and his family sat together trying to list all the states. They wrote down every state that everyone in the family could remember, and came up with forty-seven. They tried alphabetizing to see what they were missing, but the list stubbornly stood at forty-seven.

Then, some time after midnight, through the silent apartment and echoing out into the empty city street, a loud yell came from twelve-year-old George's room.

"Colorado!"

Everyone laughed and then went back to sleep. Nobody ever forgot Colorado again.

Laughter can diffuse a difficult situation. My brothers, sisters, and I watched in horror as a disembodied hand crawled across the floor. We couldn't move, we couldn't think. Grandpa George knew he had to do something quickly. Suddenly he stepped in front of the television screen and assumed the position of a hammy vaudevillian singer. "I ain't got no-*body*" he belted out, corrupting the 1920s hit "I Ain't Got Nobody" and sending us into peals of laughter at the same time. The movie was more funny than scary after that. Grandpa knew the proverb that says, "A word fitly spoken is like apples of gold in pictures of silver," means that sometimes a difficult situation demands gold-medal humor and the resulting silver laughter.

Laughter can be contagious. The poet Ella Wheeler Wilcox, born in 1850, said it best: "Laugh, and the world laughs with you; Weep, and you weep alone…." A 2008 study done by Harvard Medical School and the University of California, San Diego, confirms her statement. The study shows that both happiness and sadness are contagious; they spread through social networks. There is a statistical relationship, not only between your happiness and the happiness of those around you, but also between your happiness and that of friends of friends of friends. Happy friends make happy friends. One of the best ways to spread happiness is through laughter. So, spread a little laughter, and make a big difference.

Laughter can change history. In 1984, Ronald Reagan was the oldest U.S. president ever to have served. When he ran again for office, he was asked during a debate whether he was up to the work because of his age. Without missing a beat, Regan said solemnly that he would not make age a political issue. "I am not," he said, "going to exploit for political purposes my opponent's youth and inexperience." The room, his opponent Walter Mondale, and the country burst into collective laughter. We don't know what would have happened if he had said something else, but we do know that this statement was a defining moment in an election that led to a landslide victory for Reagan.

Laughter can help you learn, lift your spirits, change you and those around you, and maybe even change the world. It is truly a great gift. Use it well, use it wisely, and use it often.

EXERCISE

Laugh and Remember

If you have something difficult to learn, try making a funny poem about it or a funny phrase (like a list-order acronym) that helps you remember. Or, if you are artistic, draw funny a picture or diagram. Combining laughter with something you need to remember helps your brain to hang on to the information. Here are some famous examples of these "mnemonic" (memory) devices:

★ For spelling (an example of a short poem):

"I" before "E", except after "C".
And "weird" is just weird.

- Order of taxonomy in biology (an example of a list order acronym):
  "Kingdom, Phylum, Class, Order, Family, Genus, Species"
  Kids Prefer Cheese Over Fried Green Spinach.
- The value of Pi to six digits (substitute the number of letters in the words with the number itself):
  3.141592
  How I wish I could calculate Pi!

☆

"Spread a little laughter;
make a big difference."
Jill Byington

The Gift of
LEADERSHIP

By Sujin Park

When I was nine, the world, as I knew it exploded. My dad moved our family of four to Birmingham, England. My playground had been Seoul, Korea, where my Asian playmates were cautious, quiet, focused, and obsessed with education. Suddenly, I was plunged into a metropolis populated with multi-nationals. I had never seen a black person before…nor a Pakistani, nor an Indian. Culture shock times ten!

In Birmingham, my friends hailed from every continent boasted a multitude of languages, customs, and religions. My new English playmates were less focused on school. Without the concern of living up to Korean intellectual expectations, I thrived in group activities and sports. My confidence and self-esteem escalated as I helped people from diverse backgrounds connect in a positive way through social clubs and school events. With limited financial resources, several of my new friends were hesitant to get involved. They looked to me for guidance as I assumed a leadership role. I was a star.

When I was fifteen, my dad moved us to America. I was ecstatic. California was the promised land. I couldn't wait to show the Yanks the prowess of this Korean girl with a British accent!

My bravado deflated the first day of school. In upper class Moraga, diversity is non-existent. Campolindo High School is one of the highest-ranking schools in the state for academics. I felt small, insignificant, and intimidated by the relative affluence of my fellow students. Despair filled my soul. How was I to fit in, much less excel?

Then I heard that a local charity needed volunteers. Be the Star You Are! empowers women, families, and youth through improved literacy, positive media, and tools for living. The "star" part captured my attention.

At my interview, the founder, Cynthia Brian, asked if I'd like to join the Star Teen Book Review Team.

"No" I responded, " I don't like to read."

"Would you like to write for our newsletter?" I was asked.

"No, I don't like to write."

"Hmmm, what do you like to do?" was the next question. Looking around the office strewn with books, I suggested organizing.

"Done!" said the director.

That day began the rest of my story. While organizing, I ventured to read a book. Astonishingly I enjoyed it! Interacting with the book reviewers, I wrote a review. Reading, writing, and getting published became passions. I was actually good. My confidence rose.

I volunteered for more responsibilities. Soon, I was teen chairperson, overseeing the book reviewers, delegating volunteers for events, organizing the office, and updating inventories. From shipping resources for disaster relief to supplying books to juvenile halls, the homeless, abused, and forgotten, I discovered the paradox of life: when we serve others, we serve ourselves. I had blossomed into an unstoppable leader.

Shortly, I will search for another "me" to train as teen chairperson. Be the Star You Are! offered me the assurance that I am enough with the ability to shine no matter where I reside in this world.

Success is not dependent on the color of your skin, the slant of your eyes, the city you live in, or the God you worship. Success is dependent on your determination to assimilate, cooperate, and initiate.

The stringent academic standards at Campolindo with its exceptional student body reacquainted me with the desire to excel scholastically and socially. I intend to share my unique gifts as I embark on my next adventure. We are all stars.

I am proud to be a Korean girl with a British accent from California on her way to New York City. Seoul or Birmingham, Moraga, or New York. The world is my playground. I know the game. It's time to play.

EXERCISE

Grow Your Leadership

To start the leadership exercise, I invite you to answer the following questions.

- ★ What are your greatest fears?
- ★ What one thing could you do to overcome those fears
- ★ What motivates you?
- ★ To you, what does it mean to be a leader?

- ★ Think about three things you are good at. It is helpful to write them down as you are thinking.
- ★ Why do think you are good at this?
- ★ Who could benefit when you share your skills?
- ★ List three specific things you could do right now to help others, using your unique skills, gifts, and abilities. Write down who, when, and how.

This exercise not only brings about more confidence, but it also lets you discover your skills that you were not aware of. Here are three tips to grow your leadership qualities.

- ★ Be confident! Try not to think about what others would think about you.
- ★ Do not pay attention to your weaknesses. Focus on things you are good at and tell yourself that you are the best.
- ★ Always listen to other people's opinions. It is very important to be able to listen to others if you want to be a leader.

☆

"Fail to honor people, they fail to honor you;
but of a good leader who talks little,
when his work is done, his aim fulfilled,
they will all say, "We did this ourselves".
Lao Tzu

The Gift of LETTING GO

By Pat Stone

Our changing community took another step towards growing up when our brand-new school opened. That same day my youngest son, eleven-year old Tucker, took another step towards growing up as well. He was the first student ever to go to Cane Creek Middle School.

How do I know? Well, on that very first morning at five-dark-thirty, Tucker and I pulled into the completely empty school parking lot determined to make the *Guinness*—or at least, Fairview—*Book of Records.* We brought a blanket, flashlight, juice bottle, and book of *Jack Tales* for me to read aloud. And we pitched camp right outside the door.

We weren't there a half-hour before the head custodian showed up. Don, a kindly man who likes to lead three-day trail rides over the mountain range near our house, let us in so we could sit in the cafeteria. There I read Tucker "Jack and the Doctor's Girl" and "Jack and King Marock" and "Jack and Sop Doll". After all, we had some time to kill.

A week before that, I had taken my oldest daughter, seventeen-year old Jesse, down to Chapel Hill, North Carolina for her three-day freshman orientation. The school made no bones about the reality of the coming separation. "When you bring your student down to move her in, be sure not to get in any arguments about how she decorates her room. You don't want your last words together to be hostile ones. And don't linger around; she needs to start adjusting to being on her own. Help her unload—and then leave."

A month before that, my oldest son, Nate, and I had a discussion about what he was going to do after the coming school year, his last in college. I took the clinging parent role: "Well, you're always welcome to stay here as long as you want. This is home, you know." He, quite gently this time, took his perennial *I'm-going-to-get-out-of-this-place* stance. Then I loaded him and his stereo in our pick-up truck and drove him down to Atlanta so he could spend the summer having his long-desired experience of living on his own in an inner city. We finally found him a room—right between a college and a crack house.

Then there's Sammy, our fifteen-year-old, who lives for the day when she gets her license and can go places on her own. "Need to pick up some stamps, Dad? I'll drive!" "Let's go rent a movie! I'll drive!"

Back to Tucker. We were taking a short break from *Jack Tales* (to rest my voice), when, one by one, other new Cane Creekers began showing up in the cafeteria and, silent and nervous, grabbing seats. I became aware that sitting there with a blanket, etc., might be a little awkward for Tuck, so I suggested we walk outside and put the things in the truck. When we got outside, I asked him, "Tuck, do you want me just to put these things in the truck myself and come back here to you, or would you rather I go on home?"

"I don't care, Dad."

"I'll do either one. Which would you prefer?"

"Either one's fine."

"No, Tucker, this is your decision. I don't mind either way. What do you want?"

Then, very softly, he said, "Well, maybe you could go."

Down at that University of North Carolina orientation, one of the no-no's we learned was "Don't ever tell your child, 'These are the best years of your life.'" I understand the temptation. I loved college. It was fun and exciting and anxious and new. Everything felt so important, so full of possibilities. If someone came up and offered me a chance to head back in time, I'd go back to then, no doubt about it.

But the best years of my life? No, I wouldn't trade all the ones I have had then for a single day I've had as a parent. Not one.

EXERCISE

Letting Go is Hard to Do

For teens, remember this is an emotional time for your parents who have spent your lifetime nurturing you. As parents, seeing your babies grow up into strong confident teenagers is both joyous and sad. Joyous because you have raised them to be self-sufficient, sad because you know the day is near where they will soon be leaving the nest. Give the kids wings.

Teens, be gentle with your folks. Let them know you appreciate their caring, and make sure to put mom and dad on speed dial. Then spread your wings and fly!

☆

"Let go and every day will be the best day of your life!"
Cynthia Brian

The Gift of
LOVE

By Heather Brittany

How often do we take life and the people we love for granted? As humans, we tend to believe that what makes life fulfilling is money and material objects. In actuality, it is the power of love that is expressed between people that is the most important. When we are young, we feel entitled to have it all. We tend to live fast, on the edge, as if there is no tomorrow. And guess what? There may not be a tomorrow. The time we waste being angry with our parents because of all the rules and regulations they put upon us is time better spent learning more about them and loving for them for who they are. Because, as I found out when I went away to college, those rules were not to punish me but to protect me. My parents loved me above all else.

Growing up, I had a close friend, Megan, who lived next door. As little kids, we planned our futures together, talked about going to college and the type of boy we would marry. All that goopy gooey girl stuff. Of all the numerous subjects we discussed, death was never among them. The winter of our freshman year in high school, Megan had a bad headache at school and went to the nurse's office to call her dad to take her home. Before he arrived, Megan died of a brain aneurysm. It was one of the most devastating moments of my life. My young friend was gone, and I'm not sure I had ever told her how much our friendship meant to me. What I realized that day is the importance of expressing yourself today, because death does not wait for us to show our love.

The world turns…with or without us. Each individual life is a brief flash on this star called Earth. So while we inhabit this universe in this body, the greatest gift we can give ourselves is to value our own being and to share our life with another. Love is the most powerful emotion the human psyche produces. When we take time to appreciate each other, we experience true enlightenment and self-fulfillment. Often, humans do not express their feelings until the death of a loved one. Don't wait for a tragedy or the somber moment of death to realize that it is people who make our joy.

EXERCISE

Love Lessons

Today, write a card to every person you love to let them know just how you feel. It doesn't have to be long, a few words of endearment will do. In fact, "I love you" is only three words. And don't forget to write a card to yourself. Love yourself first, and you'll have the ability to love others.

☆

"Love one another. Love deeply.
Love. You are precious."
Heather Brittany

The Gift of NOW

By Davis Lunsford

I received my jersey with delight. It was blue, with *Angels* printed in white letters. I wore it proudly during my first season in Tee-Ball. That was the start of a seven-year stint in Little League baseball.

The following spring I played Tee-Ball again, but I found myself looking forward to the next season, when I would move up to Machine-Pitch. In Machine-Pitch, not only did the pitch move when someone hit it, but those seven-year-old big kids could actually put their gloves in front of their faces *before* the ball got there. I had only begun to master that skill, but after a year in Machine-Pitch I had perfected it. I couldn't wait to move on to Kid-Pitch.

Kid-Pitch presented more excitement-like learning to discern between balls and strikes, and occasionally trying to dodge a wild pitch. When I did get pegged though, it wasn't so bad. It was the most reliable way for me to get on base, and my dad had thrown enough wild pitches in batting practice that I was used to the pain. After my games I'd get a Frito Pie and a Coke and go over to the Eleven-and-Twelve-Year-Old field to watch the older kids play. I'd gawk whenever one of them belted a ball over the eight foot "Green Monster". I was happy when I moved up to the Eleven-And-Twelve-Year-Old division, but at that level the "Green Monster" didn't look half as daunting as the huge Pony League field on which the oldest Little Leaguers played.

In Little League, no matter what level I was at, the next level was the one I anticipated. Beneath me the little kids *played*; above me the older kids *competed.* Most peoples' thoughts follow that blueprint. Junior-High students want to attend high school; high-school students want to go to college. Fifteen-year-olds want to drive; sixteen-year-olds want cars. We naturally anticipate the next level. However, when we reach it, we look again for what's next.

Teenagers are especially prone to look ahead. Teenagers' lives change fast, and colleges and careers approach rapidly.

Stop looking ahead so hard that you miss the now. *Now* is the time you can control most. Enjoy where you are; you'll only be there for so long. Keep a watchful eye on the future, but have fun, work hard, and grow morally in the present.

Adolescence has been defined as a brief biological process, a seven-year time span. Modern teenagers face adult-size capabilities and child-size cultural expectations. You can either validate those low expectations, or you can dispel them. Because you probably don't have to care for a family or work full-time, you can explore opportunities that may never come again. You can pick the path you want to walk and start walking. Our culture presents teenagers with a time when they can decide what they want to do and who they want to be. Make those decisions count because it's the preparation of today that determines the success of tomorrow.

It's natural to desire to move on to the next big thing, but *right now* only happens once, so put your effort into the present. Keep your eye on the ball, not on the next field.

EXERCISE

Write Now!

Take five minutes every day and journal. Record what you think, feel, or do. Writing down your daily experiences will help you pause and appreciate them. Eventually, you'll have a record you'll enjoy re-reading. A journal, while keeping you focused on the present, will allow you to review the past and articulate your vision for the future.

☆

"The preparation of today determines the success of tomorrow."
Davis Lunsford

The Gift of OPTIMISM

By Bud Bilanich

Mark Twain once wrote, "All you need is ignorance and confidence, and success is sure." He may have been joking, or he may have serious. Regardless, here's a story that shows that Mark Twain was right—at least as far as I was concerned.

When I was in high school, I was interested in writing. I was the editor of my school's paper and yearbook. In the spring of my junior year, the local newspaper, *The Beaver County Times*, announced a contest. The winners would get a scholarship to the High School Press Institute's summer program at Kent State University. All you had to do was write an essay about why you should be picked for the scholarship.

This sounded like a good deal to me. I would get to spend two weeks on a college campus, living in the dorms. I'd learn about more about writing and newspaper production. I'd meet kids from all over western Pennsylvania and Ohio. I'd get away from caddying for a couple of weeks. And, most important, I'd get to meet girls who were from a different town than my own. You bet I was going to enter the contest.

I also was pretty confident that I would win. Being the editor of my high school paper and yearbook, I knew that I was one of the two best writers in my high school. I was fairly confident that I would write one of the two best essays.

I worked really hard on my essay because I really wanted to win. I was proud of what I wrote. As I put it in the mailbox, I knew that I had written the very best essay I could. Coupled with the fact that I knew the other kids who might be competing against me, I was pretty confident.

Sure enough, about a month later, I answered the phone and the voice on the other end of the line said, "Congratulations, Bud Bilanich, you're one of two high school students from all of Beaver County who has won a scholarship to the High School Press Institute's summer program at Kent State."

Now there was a surprise! I misunderstood the rules of the contest. I thought that two students from each high school would win; not two students from the entire county. There were about thirty high schools in our county at that time. My odds of winning were a lot lower than I thought they were. Yet I still won.

Getting back to Mark Twain and his ideas about ignorance and confidence…I was ignorant of the contest rules. As I was writing my essay, I thought my chances were pretty good because I knew I was one of the two best writers in my high school. This gave me the confidence not only to enter the contest, but also to write my best essay.

Had I known that I was competing with kids from over thirty high schools, I might not have been as confident when it came to writing my essay. This lack of confidence might have led to a more timid essay—and not winning the scholarship.

There is a common-sense point here, and it's called optimism. Optimists are people who look on the more favorable side of events and expect good things to happen. As in my case, sometimes a little ignorance of the difficulty of a challenge helps you to be more optimistic.

President Obama is an optimist. I was inspired to work on his campaign after I read his book *The Audacity of Hope.* Optimists choose hope. I do, and I hope you do too. Barack Obama put it this way. "(Hope is) the gall to believe that, despite personal setbacks such as the loss of a job or an illness, we have some control—and therefore responsibility—over own fate."

I choose optimism, hope, and personal responsibility. I hope you do too as you go through life. If you take advantage of the gift of optimism, you're likely to become a big success.

Since I was a boy, I have had this framed on my wall. Embrace it!

The Optimist Creed

Promise Yourself:

- ★ To be so strong that nothing can disturb your peace of mind.
- ★ To talk health, happiness, and prosperity to every person you meet.
- ★ To make all your friends feel that there is something in them.
- ★ To look at the sunny side of everything and make your optimism come true.
- ★ To think only of the best, to work only for the best, and to expect only the best.

- ★ To be just as enthusiastic about the success of others as you are about your own.
- ★ To forget the mistakes of the past and press on to the greater achievements of the future.
- ★ To wear a cheerful countenance at all times and give every living creature you meet a smile.
- ★ To give so much time to the improvement of yourself that you have no time to criticize others.
- ★ To be too large for worry, too noble for anger, too strong for fear, and too happy to permit the presence of trouble.

EXERCISE

Be an Optimist

- ★ Write down ten things that you think you cannot accomplish.
- ★ Identify the difficulties in accomplishing what you want.
- ★ Find the opportunity in each of the identified difficulties.
- ★ Take advantage of the opportunities, and accomplish that which you thought you could not.
- ★ Be optimistic and know you will succeed when you do your best.

☆

"A pessimist sees the difficulty in every opportunity.
An optimist sees the opportunity in every difficulty."
Winston Churchill

The Gift of ORGANIZATION

By Cynthia Brian

We live in a disposable society, and almost everyone collects too much junk. Rather than wearing things out, we either throw them away or jam them in a closet, creating more clutter. Being unorganized creates a life of chaos where you can't find something when you really need it. This in turn has a negative psychological effect which makes you feel insecure and out of control. When you organize your personal space and keep your place clean, you feel more in charge of your life.

Recently, when Heather was looking for students to share her house with her, she had to clean out rooms and closets to make space for the new roommates. As she went through her clothes, she realized she had so many items that she no longer wore, wanted, or fit into that were just taking up space. Boxes went to Goodwill and other organizations. I flew to San Diego to help sort, reorganize, and clean. The result was not only a sparkling beautiful home, but, with the uber-organization, everything has a place and is easier to find.

A teen client of mine felt stuck for a very long time. She rarely finished what she started, she missed appointments because she failed to keep a calendar, her grades were falling at school because she misplaced assignments, and she often lost items, especially clothing. Her parents were exasperated with her ineptitude, and she was rapidly descending into depression. Within a couple of coaching sessions, we realized that the root cause of her problems was her predisposition to be disorganized. Her messy habits were sabotaging her happiness.

It wasn't a fatal flaw. Learning how to be organized is an ongoing process. If you are having trouble turning in homework or can't see the floor of your room because of all the clothes, papers, and junk littering the area, here are a few tips to make order out of chaos.

★ File, don't pile. Use a desktop filing system to label and store current class assignments. All papers need to be filed for later use, tossed, or dealt with immediately.

★ Buy three ring binders or accordion folders and put all those loose papers inside according to subject.

★ Write down all assignments in a planner with times due. Make sure to note any meetings, engagements, or after-school activities.

- ★ Create a workspace that is solely yours in your room. Remove all the CD's, DVD's, games, and magazines, and neatly put them on a shelf or in a drawer.
- ★ When you remove your clothes, hang them up or put them in the wash, but don't throw them on the floor to do later. Later never comes and the bigger the mess, the more difficult it is to begin to clean it.
- ★ Don't try to clean out all drawers, closets, or rooms at one time. Decide on a small area and complete the task. Feel the success.
- ★ Make "to do" lists. When you see something in writing, it registers in your brain. Check your lists the night before school or engagements.

You have the power to purge the procrastination, edit the treasures, and get organized. When you do, you'll feel less stress, enjoy more harmony, and find more time to relax and play. Learn to be organized as an adolescent and you will reap rewards as an adult. Get rid of the things that are not bringing you pleasure and you'll make room for things that do. Start today.

EXERCISE

Spring Cleaning

Spring-cleaning isn't just a cliché. It's a necessity. Start in your bedroom by donating or selling any clothing in your closet that doesn't fit you or you don't like. Keep only things that flatter and that you wear. Next attack your desk. Open that top drawer. What do you see? Yikes! Use the folder, binder, and file system outlined above. Pick up all the junk on the floor. Vacuum, dust, and re-arrange your room for comfort. Go through your backpack and throw away the wrappers, broken pencils, and garbage that has been collecting throughout the year. Buy the proper containers for your items. Grab the broom and dustpan. Clear out your locker. Create space and a place for everything. Shine up your life by eliminating clutter. There is meaning in cleaning.

☆

"For a life of balance and well-being,
clean the clutter and get organized."
Cynthia Brian

The Gift of PERSISTENCE

By Cynthia Brian

"Giving up" are two words not in my vocabulary. When I was growing up on the farm, the eldest of five children, money was scarce, while love and encouragement were in abundance. We all worked on the ranch, picking fruit, driving the tractor, and caring for the animals, each according to our age and skill level. I didn't attend pre-school or kindergarten because they didn't exist in our area. At the age of six and three-quarters, I started first grade where I quickly became enthralled with reading, writing, and learning. As I gained knowledge, I raced home each day to share it with my siblings, helping them learn to read and write before they began their schooling.

Our teacher talked about an institution of higher learning called "college" one day in second grade. That night at dinner I announced to my parents that I wanted to go to college. They looked at one another and agreed that it would be a great opportunity. However, there was a slight caveat. I would need to figure out a way to earn enough money to finance my own education. No one in my family had ever attended college before.

For weeks we brainstormed how I would accomplish this feat, until finally I had the answer. I would raise chickens and sell the eggs. To my young mind, I reckoned that everyone ate eggs. At the ripe old age of eight, I became the Chicken Lady with a dozen Rhode Island Red pullets and a rooster named Chanticleer. I joined 4-H and was the sole member of the poultry project, teaching myself the skills of fowl husbandry.

As soon as my hens began producing, customers lined up to buy my farm-fresh eggs—fifty cents for large, forty cents for medium, and thirty cents for small. Once my dad understood that I was serious about my new venture, he built me larger coops, allowing me to breed and buy more hens, which led to more egg production. Every morning I'd rise at 5:00 AM, don my dad's World War II army jacket over my pajamas, and head to the chicken coops to feed and water the chickens, collect, clean, weigh, and box eggs before leaving for school at 7:00 AM. After school each day, my Mom would drive me around to deliver my eggs. Then I'd return to the coop in the evening to do it all over again.

I entered my chickens and Chanticleer in county and state fairs and soon was winning blue ribbons. With more exhibitions and shows under my belt, Cynthia's chickens were becoming quite well known. Chanticleer and I were a great team, and he won Grand Champion at every event, helping me become California's Champion Rooster Raiser.

Despite the raids by fox, raccoon, weasel, skunk, and mountain lion, which diminished my cherished flock, as well as freezing and hot spells, which killed many birds, I persisted. I hated getting up so early 24/7, but I was on a mission to go to college. My desire to sleep in earned me the mocking familial title of "Princess". I budgeted carefully, foregoing personal luxuries and opened a savings account to deposit every extra penny that wasn't spent on chicken expenses. In high school, I learned to sew as another 4-H endeavor so that I could make my own clothes, thus saving more money. Even though those aren't titles one would usually choose as a teenager, it didn't bother me that my nickname was "The Chicken Lady" or "The Egg Lady". Since I was the captain of the cheerleading squad and our school mascot was the falcon, we named one of my hens Freddie Falcon, and she became our good luck charm, attending the games in her "chicken costume".

By my senior year, those first twelve chickens increased to over two thousand. By the time I was eighteen, I had earned enough money from selling eggs to finance my entire university experience. It wasn't easy, and there were many days that I wanted to give up. The never-ending work was not glamorous, the poop had to be scooped, the coop had to be rebuilt, and the hens needed constant care. Yet, by keeping my end goal in mind, I was able to carry on even on the darkest days. I am proud that I didn't give up when the going got tough. My chickens provided me with an irreplaceable education at the Université de Bordeaux, University of California at Los Angeles (U.C.L.A.) University of Hawaii, and Cal, Berkeley.

Today, I am still known as "The Chicken Lady" and "The Egg Lady" because I still have a cottage industry of raising a variety of free-range hens to provide farm fresh eggs though they now sell for ten times more to grateful customers. Moreover, I went from chicken poop to chicken coop, to being a *New York Times* best selling author of *Chicken Soup for the Gardener's Soul.* That chicken manure certainly makes great fertilizer!

EXERCISE

Sunny Side Up

Whatever you want in life, you can have if you are willing to work long and hard to achieve it. Dream the dream, write your plan, get the skills you need, go into action, find a support person, and believe in yourself and all the possibilities. You don't have to raise chickens or have a blue-ribbon rooster like Chanticleer, but you do have to have a dream. When the going gets tough, just keep on going. Carry on!

The following poem has helped me throughout most of the detours in my life. Whenever I'm ready to throw in the towel, I re-read this advice. Let it guide you to success.

Don't Quit

When things go wrong, as they sometimes will,
When the road you're trudging seems all up hill,
When the funds are low, and the debts are high,
And you want to smile, but you have to cry,
When care is pressing you down a bit,
Rest if you must, but don't you quit.
Life is queer with its twists and turns,
As everyone of us sometimes learns,
And many a failure turns about,
When he might have won had he stuck it out.
Don't give up though the pace seems slow,
You may succeed with another blow.
Success is failure turned inside out,
The silver tint of the clouds of doubt,
And you never can tell how close you are.
It may be near when it seems so far.
So stick to the fight when you're hardest hit.
It's when things seem worse
That you must not quit.
—Anonymous

Turn on your chicken chatter and be tenacious.

☆

"Persistence prevails when all else fails.
Never ever give up on your dreams!"
Cynthia Brian

The Gift of POSITIVITY

By Ivan Burnell

Being positive about your life is a gift that no one else can give you. You must give it to yourself. No one else can, no matter how much they want to. Has anyone ever told you that you can have whatever you want? Could you possibly believe that? Or do you believe that you will have to settle for something less? Well, what is it that you *really* want? Oh, sure, you want to ace that chemistry test next week, or you want a terrific date for the prom, or you want to get a positive acceptance from the college of your choice. Are those just dreams? Or are they something you really want?

Real wants are defined. Determined desires are specific. When you get them, you recognize them, and just as important, you know why you want them. In my courses, at the first session, I usually ask each participant to write down what they want in their life, for today, tomorrow, next year, and the next decade. Nearly everyone starts by writing that they just want to be happy. Yet most of them cannot define what would make them happy. Their assignment (and yours also) is to define exactly what they want in detail for different areas of their life and why they want it.

Let me tell you the story of Anna. She was nineteen when she attended my course hoping to learn skills that would help her be more positive and create a life of happiness. She knew that eventually she wanted to marry, but because she lived in a small town of less than five hundred people, she was discouraged by the scarcity of decent young bachelors. Most of the marriages she had witnessed with the townspeople were not happy. She did not want to suffer the same fate. I had her make a list of all the characteristics that she wanted in a life partner and write down why each of those characteristics was important to her. The list became long and detailed as she worked on it. Part of her assignment was to read the list over each day. As she did this, she found that there were some areas in her own life that needed improvement. She showed me the list, and I encouraged her to continue dreaming.

However, she made the mistake of showing the list to some girlfriends. They laughed at her and told her that there was no one like the person she described in her dream book living in this town. "You'll have to settle for someone else, just like the rest of," they told her. Anna continued clarifying her vision and improving herself, determined to create her destiny. One day, a young single man moved into that town and they became friends. Was it "good luck " that he fit the description on her list? Or was it because she was prepared to recognize the qualities in someone else that she had also developed within herself? Today they are happily married!

Of course, you don't have to get married to lead a complete and happy life. A healthy marriage is what Anna wanted. When you are positive you can have what you want too. Start by writing a list of what you want. Be specific as to what you want and why you want it. Do you want an "A" in that test next week? What are you going to do to get it? "Good luck" happens to those who are prepared and ready to accept their good fortune.

EXERCISE

Attract Positivity

What do you really want to attract into your life? Take a few moments and write down in detail everything that would make you very happy and fulfilled. What does it look like, how does it feel, who is with you? Use your senses to express your ideas and feelings. The Law of Attraction is no secret. Believe in the possibilities of manifestation, and decide to attract only positive outcomes.

☆

"Be careful what you ask for.
You will eventually get it. Think positive!"
Ivan Burnell

The Gift of POSSIBILITY

By T J Hoisington

Achievers know exactly what they want and consistently move toward it, believing that the goal they seek is possible. Then, when great opportunities manifest themselves, achievers realize they were not simply a coincidence, but part of the design.

For years I had wanted to write a book. Daily, I would 'dwell' on the attainment of that goal. Then one night I was listening to a thirty-year-old audiotape of the best selling author and motivational speaker, Charlie "Tremendous" Jones. While listening, I noticed a phone number that was printed on the cassette tape label. I thought to myself, "I wonder if this phone number is still active?" It was eleven o'clock at night when I dialed the phone number, and it began ringing. Then, just as I was about to hang up, someone answered. The low voice on the other end said, "Who is this?" In response I said, "Who is this?" After a short pause, I gave him my name. I then asked, "May I ask with whom I am speaking?"

"This is Charlie 'Tremendous' Jones."

Surprised I said, "You've got to be kidding me! This is *the* Charlie 'Tremendous' Jones?"

He said, "That's me!"

I asked, "Where do you live?"

He said, "Pennsylvania."

I quickly apologized. "Please tell me I didn't wake you up."

"Oh, no," he replied.

I said, "In Pennsylvania, it's one o'clock in the morning," and I inquired why he was up at that hour. He proceeded to tell me he was reading one of his many books. I remember chatting with him for probably forty minutes or so as he shared some advice about writing a book. Years later, not long after my first book was published Charlie "Tremendous" Jones" called me up and ordered 25,000 copies of my book. This experience was not simply a coincidence!

Months later, I was in southern California when I was reminded that the office of the renowned author and speaker Brian Tracy's was near where I was staying. After downloading the directions from the Internet, I drove to his office, hoping for a tour. When I arrived, the secretary was puzzled. She said she had never had such a request before, and that she would need to speak to her supervisor. When she stood up to leave, I asked her if Brian Tracy frequently came in the office. She said, "Normally, no."

The word "normally" came off her lips a little hesitantly, so I inquired about her use of the word. She responded, "Typically, when Mr. Tracy comes into town from being on the road, he works out of his home so he can spend as much time as possible with his family." I immediately asked if I could meet Mr. Tracy. She said she wasn't sure and left to ask her supervisor.

Two minutes later the president walked up and asked how he could help me. I explained that I wanted a tour of the office and, "Since Mr. Tracy is in the office, I'd love to meet him, too." He told me he would see what he could do. Two minutes later, I remember looking down the office hallway and seeing Brian Tracy walk right toward me with his hand out to shake mine.

"Hi, I'm Brian Tracy."

I said, "Hi, I'm TJ Hoisington." We visited for a few minutes, and he gave me a tour of his office. Before I left, I told Mr. Tracy that I had recently begun writing a book and asked if he would be willing to read the manuscript and write an endorsement.

He thought for a moment and said, "I'd be happy to..."

Both these high achievers, and many more since, have endorsed my books and helped me with my own success. Experiences like these are all made possible because I knew exactly what I wanted. I believed in the goal and myself—and I consistently acted on ideas and impressions. You can create your own *gift of possibility* and *success* with the same simple formula.

EXERCISE

Yes, You Can!

Think of something that you really want to happen that would have a positive result for everyone concerned. Write that goal in a notebook or journal. Give it a date when you would like to see it accomplished. Perhaps you want to learn to play a musical instrument, and you have a favorite artist. Do research on the artist, write him/her a letter, or pick up the phone and call. Make sure to be clear on what you desire and decide to take the appropriate actions to make your dreams come true. You have the power to create your future. You are an achiever. Believe in the possibilities because *Yes*, you can!

☆

"We are all living in cages with the doors wide open."
George Lucas

The Gift of READING

By Cynthia Brian

Books have always been my trusted companions. As a child, I loved *The Wind in the Willows* and the Beatrix Potter series. During pre-adolescence, it was the *Lives of the Saints, Nancy Drew, Anne of Green Gables,* and *The Hardy Boys.* During my teens years, I sought comfort in biographies, histories, Jane Austen, the Bronte sisters, Shakespeare, and romance...lots of romance. Serious reading was part of my university education with books on anthropology, geography, history, art, theatre, philosophy, religion, and geology combined with the occasional personal growth tome. Besides books on achievement and self-help, my current fascination is the exploits of the wayward sailor, Tristan Jones, who beautifully writes about his adventures and mishaps on incredible voyages on the Seven Seas in a small craft.

There was never a time that I didn't have a book on my bedside table.

During time of turmoil, I turn to books. Books have their own unique power. They allow us to get inside the lives of characters and lose ourselves in an adventure in a way that movies, the Internet, or real life cannot. Books last for generations, and never lose their appeal. They are the gift that keeps on giving. There are the perennial favorites like *Little Women, Gone with the Wind*, and *The Wizard of Oz* that continue to amuse me, no matter how many times I've read them. As I coach my young students today, I find they are enraptured with the *Harry Potter, Vampire Knight,* and *Twilight* series.

It doesn't matter what you read, just as long as you spend some time every day reading. The more you read, the better you'll write and converse. Your vocabulary increases and your understanding of the world grows.

I received an email this week from the President of the Authors Guild, Roy Blount, stating that he had been talking to booksellers who report that times are hard. Here's an edited snippet of his observation.

> Booksellers aren't known for vast reserves of capital, so a serious dip in sales can be devastating. Booksellers don't receive congressional attention. A government bailout isn't in the cards. We don't want bookstores to die. Authors need them, and so do neighborhoods. So let's mount a book-buying splurge. Get your friends together and have a book-buying party. Buy the rest

> of your Christmas and holiday presents, but that's just for starters. Clear out the mysteries, wrap up the histories, beam up the science fiction! Round up the westerns, go crazy for self-help, say yes to the university press books! Get a load of those coffee-table books, fatten up on slim volumes of verse, and take a chance on romance! There will be birthdays in the next twelve months; books keep well; they're easy to wrap: buy those books now. Buy replacements for any books looking raggedy on your shelves. Stockpile children's books as gifts for friends who look like they may eventually give birth. Hold off on the flat-screen TV and the GPS (they'll be cheaper after Christmas) and buy many, many books.

Yes, yes, yes!

As a charity dedicated to improving literacy, Be the Star You Are! provides an online bookstore where you can find many of your favorite books at a deep discount. Visit http://www.amazon.com/shops/be_the_star_you_are_charity. Since the early 1990's, I have been reading three or four books a week, and in 1998 I began producing a weekly radio show, *Starstyle-Be the Star You Are!*, interviewing authors in a variety of genres. You can tune in and hear the voices of the masters. Visit http://www.cynthiabrian.com for schedules or listen to the archives at http://www.starstyleradio.com. Research has shown that you can tell the success of a person by the number of books in his personal library. When you read, you succeed.

In January of 2008, Librarian of Congress James H. Billington appointed children's book author, Jon Scieszka as the first National Ambassador for Young People's Literature. The position was created to raise national awareness of the importance of young people's literature as it relates to lifelong literacy, education, and the development and betterment of the lives of young people. Mr. Scieszka, stated, " The paperback book is still one of my favorite pieces of technology. It's portable, and you can tell how far along you are just by the feel in your fingertips."

My children still have most of my childhood literary treasures. Although my copy of *Good Night Moon* was worn and torn, they enjoyed the story as much as I had when I was a babe. Books never lose their charm, and there is always something for everyone, even the reluctant child who says he hates to read. Promoting reading and literature among young people is important for the health and creativity of our democratic society.

Literacy comes wrapped in various packages. Find a topic you enjoy. Then visit your local bookseller or library to discover a plethora of books guaranteed to ignite your passion during a long winter's night or a summer day at the beach.

Find an interesting book and dive into the pages. You'll soon realize that what's old is new again. History does repeat itself. Most important remember this fact—

you will be the same person in five years except for the people you meet and the books you read. Buy a book today!

EXERCISE

B.Y.O.B. (Bring Your Own Book)

Make reading a priority for you while you are young and you'll never experience a boring day in your life. Gather two or three friends and start your own personal book club. Meet once a month to discuss your chosen literary gem and share the pleasure of reading. Start with this copy of ***Be the Star You Are! for Teens.*** Choose two or three chapters for a session, and dig deep into the stories and lessons. Debate, discuss, and discover yourself.

"To be a leader, you must be a reader.
Read, lead, and succeed!"
Cynthia Brian

The Gift of REALITY

By Cynthia Brian

During the Christmas break, Heather came home for the holidays. As always, we enjoyed lively conversations as we brainstormed topics for upcoming radio episodes. Because I coach teens and adults for acting, writing, presenting, and life challenges, I subscribe to a multitude of magazines to keep me current on the happenings of the day. Being a student, Heather doesn't spend her hard earned cash on periodicals. What she noticed within the covers of these rags was a plethora of ordinary people basking in their fifteen minutes of fame. Many had sold their souls to the devil in exchange for headlines and spotlights on sleazy so-called reality television shows.

Television watching has become a part of almost everyone's daily landscape. In 2001, the national census in India found that in many parts of the country there were more television sets than indoor plumbing? Is it any surprise that more Americans own television sets than have toilets? It's estimated that more than sixty percent of all programs contain violence, and most programming bears little resemblance to real life, although it claims to be. Unscripted TV programs cost considerably less to produce than comedies or dramas, and since the year 2000, there has been a tremendous surge in "reality" shows. Wikipedia describes *reality television* as a genre of programming which "presents purportedly unscripted dramatic or humorous situations, documents actual events, and usually features ordinary people instead of professional actors." In just two months of shooting recently, there were over 2,000 days of unscripted production days. But is reality TV really reality?

The answer is no. Although participants may not be given lines and scripts, the people who are chosen are carefully cast to cause drama and friction, and to give "great show". That means the producers are not looking for the most talented or authentic individuals, but often the most outrageous and controversial characters. Once a contract is signed, your privacy is comprised, and the things you do or say may be taken out of context and edited to fit any situation. At what cost to your reputation and integrity are you willing to gain a few minutes of camera time? People are so often mesmerized by gold stars, trophies, and the attention of fame, that they forget that their heroes and heroines may not be worth emulating. Of course, not all reality programming is trashy. However, when clients ask me about auditioning, I caution them about the ramifications. It may be easier to be cast on a reality TV show than to book an audition for a bona fide film, but do you really want to be famous for cheating, eating worms, or unsavory behavior? Your decision becomes your genuine reality.

The purpose of this chapter is not to discourage you from applying for reality TV appearances. I am suggesting that you use reality television as a metaphor for seeing the importance of seeking attention and recognition in real life for the right reasons. Don't be so desperate for distinction that you develop a counter-productive persona. It's easy to fall into the trap of Andy Warhol's famous "fifteen minutes of fame" by going wild, becoming trashy, being promiscuous, or getting into trouble. Seeing your name in the paper for violent deeds or behaviors of a dubious nature will not enhance your life or your career opportunities. Negative notice does not develop a positive reputation.

Maintain your self-esteem and sense of self-worth by participating in activities in the real world that build character and demonstrate integrity. Play sports, write for the newspaper, raise rabbits, dance, sing, perform in local theatre, enter speech contests, earn a black belt in karate, mow lawns, babysit, tutor, and volunteer. Living your reality means experiencing everything as it comes to you. Exist in the now. Reality is that which is, and, even if you don't believe in it, reality doesn't go away. Be celebrated for being real and living your legacy. Sincerity, high moral fiber, and excellence beget gratifying fame.

I recently came across a speech I wrote as a young teenager when I was the keynote speaker at a national teen conference. The speech was titled, "Am I For Real?" What struck me as I read the words I'd written so many years ago was that much of the angst my generation expressed as teens is so similar to the yearnings of today. Our reality was that the older generation made rules we didn't understand or want. I wrote:

> What do we, the teenagers of America want? We have grown up in an era of hate, violence, and injustice. I believe we are looking for ourselves. We want to pick up the pieces of a shattered world and rebuild our lives with real significance, freedom, responsibility, and openness. We want to be accepted for who we are, inside and outside, with all our weaknesses as well as our strengths. We want respect and listening ears. We want to be seen *and* heard. We want to be authentic, to be our best selves, to find peace and love within our souls.
>
> We don't want to be a phony or pretend or put on airs. We want to be someone great while accepting ourselves with all our limitations and imperfections without shame. So how are we doing? If you can truthfully

say you are on good terms with yourself, if the image your project to others is the same kind of person you believe you are, then, my friends, *you are for real!*

We don't need reality television or celebrity magazines to validate our veracity. We just need to be our genuine true selves to feel recognized and honored. You are the writer, producer, director, and star of your own reality show. Are you for real?

EXERCISE

Get Real

Are you happy with your life as it is? If money were no object, what and who would you be? Flip through a pile of magazines and tear out pages that speak to you. On poster board of any size, make a collage of your current reality, cutting and pasting photos and clipped words from the magazines. On the other side of the board, create a collage of how you want your reality to look in five years. Dream big. Place your board somewhere that you can see it everyday. Update or redesign as your reality changes and evolves.

☆

"You are the architect of your reality.
Build with truth and live in authenticity."
Cynthia Brian

The Gift of REJECTION

By Cynthia Brian

"Nothing of great value in life comes easily. The things of highest value sometimes come hard. The gold that has the greatest value lies deepest in the earth, as do the diamonds." Norman Vincent Peale, one of my favorite inspirational authors, born in 1898, wrote these truths that are amazingly appropriate today. Benjamin Franklin said that there are only two things that are definite in life—taxes and death. I want to add a third inevitable encounter—rejection.

No matter how kind, great, talented, beautiful, educated, or motivated you are, someone, somewhere, sometime, somehow will reject you. Why, you ask, is rejection a gift? The answer is because it is not what happens to you that counts. It is how you respond. You have to learn when you are young to pick yourself back up and get on the horse if you want to succeed. Babies fall down thousands of times before they learn to walk; yet they never give up. Despite the setbacks, we must take a deep breath and move on.

As an actor, I have been rejected more times than I can remember. Continually I was told, "You're too tall, you're too short, you're too pretty, you're too ugly, you're too young, you're too old, your hair is too blonde, your hair isn't blonde enough, your eyes are too blue, your eyes aren't blue enough, you have too much experience, you're not experienced enough." But do you know what? I don't remember those negations. I only remember the jobs I booked!

Rejection is one of the most distasteful words in the dictionary—refusals, repudiations, turndowns, rebuffs, renunciations, disapproval, snubbing, dissing—basically people are shouting "I don't want you! You're not good enough!"

Since it is certain that from birth until death you will be rejected, it's a great idea to make rejection your friend and learn to rebound. How high can you bounce? None of us can be right for every situation, every relationship, every job, even though we think so. When preparation meets perspiration (as my friend Mark Victor Hansen likes to say) and when the planets line up, everything may go your way. And then again, it may not.

Many people are crushed by their first rejection. A young writer I know named Stephanie shared her teenage stories of broken hearts and how she dealt with the slighting. Every time a relationship ended, she and her mom would go into the backyard and have a burial service, not for the departed boyfriend who was undoubtedly a good person just as she is, but rather for the end of the romance. They'd dig a hole and place a photo, an old basketball schedule, a dried flower, or some memento of the romance and loss inside, then cover it with dirt with a rock and place a rock on top. After a good cry, she felt better and less rejected. The remedy was to allow time to grieve by burying her sadness at being rebuffed. She could then get on with her life. What a terrific ritual.

We won't get out of this world without experiencing rejection. The secret is to embrace it and never give up. Rejection is like the game of craps. For every "no" we get, we are closer to a "yes". When you are feeling down and out, it's hard to get up and get going. You will heal, you will forget, and you will forge ahead.

I include a favorite poem that has aided me mend my bumps and bruises by understanding that if I can be the last person standing, I'll make it. The author is anonymous, but his or her legacy is a great defense against rejection and of superb assistance for being the star you are. I suggest you copy it and post it in your room where you can see it everyday. And remember the message applies to both males and females.

If you think you are beaten, you are.
If you think you dare not, you don't.
If you'd like to win, but think you can't,
It's almost certain you won't.

If you think you'll lose, you've lost.
For out of the world we find
Success begins with a person's will
It's all in the state of your mind.

If you think you are outclassed, you are.
You've got to think high to rise.
You've got to be sure yourself before
You can ever win a prize.

Life's battles don't always go
To the stronger, or faster man.
Sooner or later the man who wins
Is the man who thinks he can!

Think of yourself as valuable as gold and as brilliant as the brightest diamond. It takes talent to recognize your worth. You are a shining star.

EXERCISE

Next Hole

The next time that you are rebuffed, think of Stephanie's ceremony. Dig a hole, place a reminder of the rejection in the dirt, have a good cry, then cover the hole up. Plant a flower on top to grow a new opportunity. With your personal rejection cemetery, you'll empower yourself with the knowledge that there is more to life than looking in the tiny rearview mirror. Think bigger. Move forward, and shout *next.*

☆

"Life is a numbers game. With every "no"
you are closer to a "yes"! Be next."
Cynthia Brian

The Gift of
RESILIENCE

By Cynthia Brian

My daytime was jam packed with appointments as I hurriedly dressed. I donned my favorite black pants, light blue sweater, heart and star necklace and earrings, pulled on my boots and rushed out the door. I was in high spirits, anticipating the fun group of young actors I would be coaching that afternoon. But first, there were errands to run with stops at the post office, dry cleaners, hardware store, market, gas station, and camera repair shop. Strangers smiled at me, and I smiled back. I felt airy and light.

Arriving at my studio, I quickly began sorting the handouts for the upcoming acting class. One by one the students arrived, all anxious to get their time on camera practicing their monologues. Class commenced, and we started our warm-up exercises. As I turned my back to demonstrate the newest tai chi movement, giggles erupted. I spun around to ask what was so funny. At first, no one wanted to say a thing as they used their hands to cover their mouths. "C'mon, guys, what's so funny? Let me in on the joke!" I pleaded.

A brave soul put up her hand. "Ms. Cynthia, are you starting a new fashion fad?"

"What are you talking about Samantha? You all know that I'm not into fads, just personal style."

"Well, Cynthia, your new '*personal style*' is a bit revealing, " Sam squealed as she and the other students were seized with another bout of laughter.

I glanced at my back in the mirror. Oh horror of horrors! The invisible nylon zipper remained firmly attached to the top of my pants while the remaining fabric had split from the waist down. A perfect heart shape revealed my usually unviewed bare bottom!

The kids held their breath as they awaited my reaction. The room relaxed as I burst out laughing with everyone joining me in the guffawing. "Oh my goodness," I chuckled, "that's why people I passed hollered to me, then giggled and waved when I turned around." I told the students about my numerous errands that I had made around the town with my mishap in full view! We laughed some more. Then we turned this embarrassing experience into an acting exercise.

Resiliency saved the day. I could have become angry and ashamed, but I chose to have fun with the situation. We predicted that the people who had witnessed my heart shaped folly enjoyed a lively conversation at the dinner table about the eccentric woman who runs around baring her assets. The students delivered a plethora of dialogue surrounding this event, all of it humorous and playful.

To be resilient means to bounce back quickly. Throughout life we will all encounter difficulties and circumstances requiring us to be flexible. The faster we can recover from our mishaps and turn negatives into positives, the more quickly we'll be able to move forward. It is not what happens to us that matters, but how it is how we respond. As we say in the entertainment world, acting is reacting. All life is a series of retorts.

When you are resilient, you'll laugh more, play more, and enjoy a higher degree of significance and self-esteem. That day I tied a sweater around my waist to hide my posterior, and we continued on with a lively session that even now is remembered with glee. I hope that your pants never rip in front of an audience, but if they do, you know how to handle it-be resilient, laugh it off, and keep going!

EXERCISE

Rubber Band Man

Like a rubber band, we need to learn the art of bouncing back. Just as a strong rubber band returns to its original size after being extended, we, too, have the ability to stretch and be pliant. Think of a time that something embarrassing happened to you. What could you have done differently that would have diffused the situation and helped you recover your composure more quickly? When disappointment and humiliation rear their fearsome heads, what are some ways you can be resilient and malleable? Believe you have the strength and stretchiness of a rubber band, and you'll be able to react with confidence in the most dire of situations. Bounce back!

☆

"The greatest mistake you can make is to fear mistakes.
You are more buoyant than you know!"
Cynthia Brian

The Gift of RESPONSIBILITY

By Maggie DiGiovanni

Mama was a drug dealer. She drugged us to keep us in line. Mama, though old-fashioned in many ways, thought raising her children in the proper manner could only be done with the use of drugs. For example, twice on Sunday and every Wednesday night, she and Daddy drug us to church. The preacher taught us about God and all the heavenly virtues. Mama and Daddy taught us to respect the teachings of the Bible.

Then if either of her three children received a note from the teacher, Mama drug us back to school to hear both sides of the story. Ninety-nine percent of the time she agreed with the teacher. If we had gotten too far out of the bounds of decency, we were drug to the barn for a serious "discussion."

Believing that family was everything, Mama drug her children, and a sometimes reluctant husband, to family reunions so we had a chance to get to know as many of our kin as possible. No matter how much work faced her, Mama drug out hugs, kissed our bumps and bruises, and helped build a playhouse or fort, according to which child made the request. Even if she was in her Sunday best and her child was covered in dirt, chocolate, or other grime, she drug out the belief that hugs were more important than the pretty dress she wore.

If any of her children did their chores in a halfway manner, she drug him or her back to the task, explained the proper way to do it, and insisted the work be completed. When we became adults, we knew that no job was too small to be done right.

As we grew, Mama drug each of us aside to tell us the facts of life and urge us to respect ourselves enough to say no to peer pressures. When we faced our biggest challenges, she was always there to listen and advise without judging.

At our senior proms, Mama drug Daddy along to chaperone. Because of the other "drugs" she had administered in our youth, none of us felt embarrassed to have our parents present. Instead, we felt honored.

Mama drug us other places, such as the dentist, doctor, and the hospital and comforted us with her presence. She taught us that if we broke the law when we got older, the police would be enforcing the "drug" rules, and they would be right to do so.

She drug us into respecting those around us and ourselves. Both Mama and Daddy drug us to realize that our good names were the only thing we had that couldn't be taken away. They could only be given away through careless actions.

Mama drug us to visit those less fortunate than ourselves and taught us to offer comfort in any way we could.

When cocaine, marijuana, and heroin became commonplace in the lives of those around us, she drug us to see the effects they had on people.

My siblings and I grew up in the miracle of a family filled with members who insisted we take responsibility for our actions. Each of us fell away from our teachings at least once, but like the prodigal son, we were brought back into the fold with love and joy. Though we were welcomed, we knew without doubt who had been responsible for our downfall. Each of us engineered our lives by making our own decisions and, for a brief time, those decisions had been wrong. Without this wealth of family, each of us might have ended in the depths of despair. Mama formed the center around which our lives evolved and Daddy, sometimes reluctantly, enforced the rules.

Yes, Mama's "drugs" were powerful, and she made sure she gave them to us personally and used them often. The first time she used them on any of her children was when she drug us into her arms and welcomed us into a world made of a loving family. I raised my children using liberal doses of the same drugs Mama dispensed until her death

EXERCISE

Mama's Drug Deals

Before making any move in your life:

★ Ask for guidance through prayer.

★ Have the courage to say no to a bad situation.

★ Consider whether your family will be proud of you.

★ Think about how younger siblings might see your actions.

★ Ask yourself: "Will I be satisfied with the outcome?"

There is no one else to blame. You are responsible for your behavior, actions, and results. Use Mama's drug deals for a life of accountability.

☆

"When you point a finger at others,
remember three fingers of responsibility
are pointing back at you."
Maggie DiGiovanni

The Gift of RISK

By Libby Gill

I majored in theater in college. While it didn't make me a Broadway star, it definitely taught me how to think on my feet. And, occasionally, fall flat on my face. Having gone to six different schools for my six years of high school, I'd become a shy loner by the time I got to college. Even so, on my first day as a college freshman, I was bitten by the theater bug when I saw a sign that read, "Auditions for *The Women*." You might know *The Women* as a Meg Ryan movie, but I knew it as a catty fem-fest from the 1939 film starring Joan Crawford and Rosalind Russell. I figured if I ever had a shot at getting a part in a play, an all-woman cast would help. I auditioned and got the part of—drum roll please—the dress shop girl. Okay, so it wasn't much of a part. But it was a beginning.

I was so psyched, I immediately signed up to be a theater major. Just one little wrinkle. Now that I had declared, I had to participate in the new student auditions for the entire department and faculty by performing a monologue. At this point, I'd never been in a play in my life, and I barely knew what a monologue was. But did that stop me? No siree. I marched down to the library and checked out a handful of plays. And what do you suppose I chose? Shakespeare's Lady Macbeth, of course. The perfect role for a totally inexperienced eighteen-year-old ingénue. Not.

Surprisingly, my risky theatrical debut paid off and I came in third—did I mention this was a competition?—out of the dozen students auditioning. Not bad for a newbie. But that was just the beginning. My next big stumble came when one of my professors told me I needed more work on voice. He didn't say exactly what that meant or where I should go to get it, but I was undeterred.

This time, I marched myself over to the music department and signed up for an opera class. Did I mention that I wasn't a singer? I figured I'd just warm up the old vocal chords, learn a few artsy songs, and dazzle my classmates with an aria—in Italian no less—for my final exam. Ha! I barely warbled my way through my song, forgot my lyrics, and lost the melody while the music majors looked on, trying to disguise their horror and pity for me. Major ouch.

I got a C in that class, the lowest grade of my entire college career. It not only brought down my GPA, but it also crushed my spirits. As far as I was concerned, a C didn't only mean I was a lousy singer, but a total loser. But you know what? Even though I didn't realize it at the time, later on I saw that it took guts to get up there and sing my aria with a bunch of real singers watching me. Eventually, I recognized that C for what it was—courage. I'd found the courage to take a risk, even if it meant I might fall on my face.

That's what I want you to be able to do in your life. Whether at school, in sports, or in the arts, go after something that gives you butterflies in the stomach. Take a risk. Fall flat on your face. It's the best place to be when you're ready to pick yourself up again.

EXERCISE

Risky Behavior

Here are some things you can try to build your risk-taking skills. Please understand that I'm not talking about crazy stuff like drag racing or sticking your hand in a lion's cage. I'm talking about healthy, positive risks that can expand your awareness and stretch your skills. Why not try one of the following?

- ★ Think of something you've always wanted to do, but have never tried, like snowboarding, bungee jumping, or sailing lessons. Grab a friend, parent, sibling—or all of the above—and give it a try.
- ★ Indulge in the arts by taking trombone lessons, a comedy improvisation class, or a ceramics workshop. Even if your peers don't get it or think it's nerdy, who cares? Don't be afraid to forge your own path.
- ★ Join a group or club that intrigues you. Meet some new friends and get involved in doing something good for your school or maybe even the planet.
- ★ Volunteer at an animal shelter, hospital, or place of worship. Even if you've never done any kind of community work, you might be surprised how much you'll learn and how good it feels to give back.
- ★ Set a goal for yourself that's a real stretch. Now, here's the catch: share that goal with others and ask them to help keep you accountable for reaching it.

Take that risk and good luck!

☆

"To fall flat on your face is human,
to get up divine."
Libby Gill

The Gift of SERENDIPITY

By Justin Murray

"Seek and ye shall find," says the Sermon on the Mount. I used to think it odd that the passage doesn't specify *what* ye shall find. Shall ye find that for which ye sought? Because otherwise, the search was rather pointless, wasn't it?

That attitude used to dominate all my searches, and I search for things frequently. Take a recent search, for example: it was time to go to school, and I'd lost my keys. I started my search at my desk, where I usually leave my keys.

No luck. I searched all the drawers, each shelf, the desktop, the garbage can beneath...I found thirteen pens, a stack of extra printer paper, a perfectly good set of ear buds, a long-lost copy of *Age of Empires*, and an USB 2.0 connector cable, but no keys.

Okay, so the keys weren't in my desk. Perhaps they were in my room? No, not there either. There was that book I'd been reading that had slid behind the bed, two more pens I'd forgotten I'd put in that drawer, the nice leather jacket I'd forgotten about on the hanger, and my Sperry loafers neatly in the corner where I'd never find them, but still I found no keys. I was beginning to panic now.

"Mom, have you seen my keys?" I called out.

My mother's voice came back saying, "No, I haven't seen your keys."

"Did Ava take them?" (Ava, incidentally, is a dog.)

"I doubt it, she knows not to take keys."

"Well, then where are they?" I threw my hands into the air, I let them fall slapping against my sides, and I found my keys. They were in my pocket.

Well might you say, "What a waste of time." That's exactly what I said at first, and it was the truth, but it needn't have been. Yes, the search for my keys was a waste of time, but I gleaned a lot from that search. I found where my pens had been hiding. That USB cable had been missing for a long time, too. And my iPod ear buds were wearing out; I could really make use of that other pair I'd found. And that was really a good book; I would go on to enjoy finishing it.

That is serendipity: the art of finding what you weren't looking for and realizing what a find it really is. Serendipity is surprisingly uncommon, considering the number of people who find what they aren't looking for. The fact is that most people just don't realize how valuable what they weren't looking for *is*. They never realize how much they miss; in fact, they're overjoyed when they find whatever they were seeking. They never miss what they didn't let themselves see.

You can do that too. You can walk about with your head down, overlooking the daffodils as you hunt for roses. But how much more pleasant would the search be if you just acknowledged the daffodils and enjoyed them too? There's nothing wrong with looking for roses or any other particular thing, but it does seem a criminal waste to ignore the treasures we find en route.

It's good to look for things, and it's better to find what you're looking for; but always remember that what you seek isn't the only thing worth finding, and learn to see the worth in what you find.

EXERCISE

Seek and Ye Shall Find!

Look for something difficult to find. Take a notebook, or small tape recorder and try these ideas:

★ As you look, make a note of everything interesting that you find (not necessarily physical; you can also "find" insights) that you weren't looking for.

★ At the end of your search, review your notes. How is each thing you found meaningful/useful? Make notes about the interesting things you find. You cannot note the same things as you did the first time. What's new that you missed earlier?

★ You can repeat this process as many times as you like, but keep in mind that you've never found everything. There's always a new use or lesson to be discovered. Try new searches, losing the notebook, or tape recorder. Try whatever variations work for you.

Learn to see the treasure in everything around you. Serendipity is common; the ability to recognize it is rare. The point of this exercise is to hone that ability so that everywhere you go, you make lucky finds.

☆

"When you look out for everything,
you're bound to find something."
Justin Murray

The Gift of SEXUALITY

By Cynthia Brian and Heather Brittany

What is sexuality? Most people will immediately assume we are talking about engaging in a sexual act, however, sexuality is not just about sex. From birth until death, every person is a sexual being. Sexuality defines our gender and can be a complex aspect of our personality. It is how we feel about ourselves. Sexuality is not so much about what you do, but who you are. The way we walk, talk, dress, and move as well as how we act among other people are all aspects of our sexual entity. Sexuality influences everything we experience in the world. Biologically, sexuality concerns itself with sexual contact in all its forms, sexual intercourse, and procreation. Philosophically, it deals with moral, ethical, and religious issues. Throughout history, different cultures portrayed sexuality according to the social dimensions of the time period. Developing a healthy-respect for ourselves as sexual individuals is crucial for maturity.

Yet, when it comes to talking about sex and sexuality, most teens don't know where to turn. Focusing on better communication between adults and teens is a major component of our radio segment, T42–A Mother/Daughter Brew. We want to share our views on teen sex and sexuality to help you make wise choices.

Heather's Bag

From the time we were really young, my mom read books to my brother and I that dealt with sexuality in age-appropriate language. All kids are curious. They want to know where babies come from and why mommy and daddy's bodies look differently. When parents are willing to talk openly with their children about sexual issues, it lessens the anxiety, answers nagging questions, and forms a foundation of trust. Unfortunately, not all adults are willing to talk about sex, especially during the teen years when open conversation is most crucial.

Cynthia's Bag

Although I had terrific parents, sex and sexuality were *not* among the topics of our discussions. I should have understood about reproduction from watching all our barnyard animals mating, however, it never crossed my mind that humans engaged in sexual contact to make babies. When my eldest cousin, Ronnie, was getting ready to go out on his first date, my Aunt Linda told my Uncle Bob to have "the talk." Nervous to discuss sex with a sixteen-year old, my uncle took my cousin aside and advised, "Just remember to keep your hands in your pockets." And as he walked out the door, my Aunt added, "fa la brava!", which means "be good" in Italian. This was the same admonition my mom told us as teens. Over the years, we enjoyed a hearty laugh about Ronnie being good while spending the entire evening with his hands in his pockets, but that is missing the point. The reality is that adults have a responsibility to prepare their children with the information they need to make educated decisions. Many parents are as fearful as their teenagers when it comes to speaking about sexuality.

Heather's Bag

I would venture to say that the majority of teenagers are uncomfortable talking with their parents about their sexuality, and vice versa. In some households, discussing anything sexual is considered taboo, sometimes because of religious beliefs. Unfortunately, if a teen can't speak to a trusted adult, he or she will get their information from a friend, who may actually provide misleading or incorrect advice. My recommendation for teens is that if you feel you can't talk to your parents, or you do not have parents in your household, confide in an adult you can trust. Go to your school nurse, an older sibling, aunt, uncle, or even a coach.

Cynthia's Bag

When teens come to my office to talk to me, my goal is always to help them understand that sexuality is a natural and healthy part of living. I answer their questions honestly and encourage them to include their parents in their concerns and questions. Often I've had an adolescent confide to me, "My parents would *kill* me if they thought I was having sex." Of course, if open communication existed in the family from early childhood, this anxiety could be avoided. It's crucial that teens become educated on the issues so that they will make wise and appropriate choices.

I vividly remember attending a state-wide sex education forum when I was a freshman in high school where students wrote their questions about sex anonymously on a piece of paper to be answered by a panel of professionals. Questions ranged from "Can I get pregnant by kissing a boy?" to "Does sex hurt?" to "How do I know when I'm ready to be sexually involved?" Other queries revolved around the development and changes happening to our bodies. Both boys and girls participated and because the questions were anonymous, no one had to risk sounding stupid. All of us left better informed, armed with information that could protect us and save us from life-altering mistakes, even if we were afraid to talk with our moms or dads.

Heather's Bag

There are no stupid questions when it comes to your health and your sexuality. Get the facts. If your parents are unapproachable, there are community health clinics you can visit that are bound by confidentiality laws. You want to feel comfortable in your body and live by your own moral values. Some teens choose to be sexually active. Others choose abstinence or wait until adulthood when they are engaged in committed relationships or marriage. Whatever you decide, you must be safe.

Cynthia's Bag

We recently interviewed a young author who wrote about her sexual exploits during her teenage years. She had felt abandoned and invisible as a child so at puberty she decided to use her physical attributes to gain popularity. She engaged in numerous "hook-ups" only to be considered a slut and not girlfriend material. Her self-esteem plummeted even more with each new sexual encounter. We also interviewed an author who wrote a best selling book about his experience being the only virgin on the popular TV show, *The Bachelor*. Even though he was teased, he was satisfied with his sexual status and had a blast dating. It's important to be true to yourself.

Being a sexual person is not about being pressured into having sex, even if everyone in your group says they are doing it. Probably a great many are exaggerating or just boasting. There is no right age to have sex. Never feel pressured and don't pressure a partner. Increase your self-confidence by recognizing that you have always been and will always be a sexual being, even when you are virgin.

Heather's Bag

The most important person to love is you. Your body and your emotions are changing and evolving rapidly throughout these teen years. Respect and honor yourself. Your sexuality is a natural and healthy part of who you are and how you live. Celebrate it.

Although neither of us is condoning or promoting sexual intimacy, we do want to make it clear that there is never a safe time to have unprotected sex. Avoid pregnancy and transmitted diseases by knowing the truth, and obtaining the tools necessary to protect yourself before you become sexually involved. There is help available at school, through organizations, community health clinics, your pediatrician, and other medical facilities. If at all possible, speak to your parents and tell them what you are feeling and experiencing. They were teenagers once.

Make healthy decisions, develop meaningful relationships, and learn to communicate your needs. Embrace your sexuality while being consistent with your personal and moral values.

EXERCISE

The Birds and the Bees

Do you know everything you need to know about sex and sexual behaviors? Have your parents or guardians had the "sex talk" with you? Make a list of your questions, then ask a trusted adult to spend some time chatting with you. Don't be embarrassed. Although every person is a sexual being, no one was born with innate sexual knowledge. Your sexuality affects your body, mind, spirit, and emotions. Treat yourself with respect and make wise decisions.

☆

"To be a human being, is to be a sexual being."
Cynthia Brian and Heather Brittany

(Editor's note: For caring, confidential consultations on sexual health, birth control, rights, and education, contact Planned Parenthood. http://www.plannedparenthood.org/ or call toll free 1-800-230-PLAN)

The Gift of SLEEP

By Pamela A. Lewis

As a child, among my least favorite words to hear my mother say was, "It's 9:00 PM: time for you to go to bed." To my young mind, those words were always spoken at the most inconvenient time. Maybe I was engrossed in some terrific show on TV, or I was reading a wonderful story. I would beg, bargain, and even try to bribe my way into an extra ten minutes of "staying up." Despite my best efforts, when it was time to go to sleep, my mother always had the final say.

When I became a teenager and entered high school, more schoolwork and a busier schedule made getting to bed early and having a good night's sleep more challenging, but no less imperative than when I was ten. But since I still lived at home and was subject to my mother's rules, I strove to turn in early (around 10:00 rather than the former 9:00) because I needed to be up by 7:00 AM the next morning and out of the house to arrive to school by at least 8:30 AM.

Although I resisted, deep down I knew that adequate sleep meant I would always feel well rested and full of the energy necessary for facing the day's activities.

Now that I am an adult and a high school teacher, sleep has become even more important for me. I am equally concerned that my students receive enough sleep so that they can learn as well as possible.

Sleep is one of the most mysterious gifts we have. Why we sleep is still unknown; however, scientific research has established that sleep is essential to a healthy life. Inadequate sleep can cause a wide range of medical problems such as depression, obesity, and heart disease. Lack of sleep can also bring about embarrassing situations. One time when a student in my school fell asleep in his history class, I happened to be passing by his classroom and noticed some of his classmates laughing and looking in at the lone, slumbering fellow slumped in his chair. The class had ended, and everyone, teacher included, had left the room. One from the laughing group took pictures of the hapless young man for some future joke. When he did wake up some moments later, he realized what had happened and was clearly embarrassed. Lack of sleep can cause you to miss out on some important moments—such as knowing when it is time to leave.

You and I live in a fascinating time with an array of technology. The Internet, cell phones and other "gadgetry" make it possible to access the news and other information twenty-four hours a day, where it happens, and as it happens. Our nights are constantly illuminated with a steady flow of lighting from streetlamps, shops, and brightly lit signs. All of these things, wonderful as they are, may put us into a state of perpetual wakefulness, throwing off our natural sleep patterns. In other words, if you are always "on," it is very hard to find time to be "off"; that is, asleep.

The gift of sleep is the gift of rest and good health, gifts that have no price because they cannot be purchased or bargained for. When you develop healthy habits and stick to them, these will be the best gifts you could ever receive.

EXERCISE

Sleeping Well

Make a list of the ways you feel or what happens when you don't get enough sleep. For example, you might list "feel tired and irritable"; "upset", etc. Then make another list of how you feel and what happens when you have had enough sleep.

Finally, list the things that you can realistically do to achieve the well being you want for yourself. Give your list to a family or close friend so that they know the goal you're trying to reach and can help encourage and support you along the way.

☆

"Sleep well for well-being."
Pamela A. Lewis

The Gift of SPORTS

By Father Patrick McGrath

At the age of twenty-four, I retired from contact competition sports. I had learned more about life on the sports field than I had in the classroom. I had known the thrill of victory and the agony of defeat, valuable lessons for the rollercoaster ride of life.

In 1968, after the assassination of Robert Kennedy and Martin Luther King, I introduced soccer into the city of Fairfield. Through sports, I wanted to give hope to the young people and to transcend culture, ethnicity, religion, and nationality. I taught the coaches in the elementary schools using a draft board (similar to chess), illustrating for them the position on the field, movements in the game, and the use of the head and without hands. It was a worthwhile project.

I became a coach. There is no letter *"I"* in the word coach. Coaching is about developing and propelling the talents of the team. My approach was to select a panel of twenty-two players, for the eleven-position squad. There was an alternative player for every position, and the ground rules were that no one was automatically in the lineup. Each player had to earn the position. Once the team was announced, the players elected a captain.

The rules were

1. Punctuality at training
2. Discipline on the pitch
3. Practice
4. Understand that you are only as good as your last training.

We followed the advice of Lou Holtz of Notre Dame who recommended that a healthy attitude toward the game was imperative. We utilized the system developed by John Wooden of U.C.L.A., who outlined building blocks for a successful team in his book *Pyramid of Success*. In creating our soccer team, we all realized that together everyone accomplishes more.

I was able to impart a value system for both soccer and life. I designed a mantra, "Care, share, and be fair." How does this work for the sport of soccer? The players know when you care about them and that you are interested in them. Because soccer is not an individual's game, players must share the ball with others. There is no room for selfishness, and being fair throughout a game is always recognized. Being fair on the field helps us to be fair in life.

If you are a soccer enthusiast, you've watched the World Cup either in person or on TV. You've cheered for the international soccer stars like Pele of Brazil, David Beckham of England, Maradona of Argentina, and Roy Keane of Ireland. Have these stars demonstrated the values we postulate of care, share, and be fair?

Sports help us learn valuable life lessons, no matter what sport you choose. Participating in a sport increases self-confidence and self worth, building positive body images while decreasing racism and school dropout rates. A study from the Women's Sports Foundation showed that high school athletes were 92 percent less likely to use drugs, 80 percent less likely to get pregnant and three times more likely to graduate than non-athletes. Friendships develop through good sportsmanship. Many of the world's greatest leaders credit sports for their business success.

Although soccer was the sport I chose to coach, any sport will help you grow as a person. Swimming, basketball, baseball, bowling, gymnastics, cycling, hurling, badminton, ping-pong, skiing, surfing, lacrosse, paintball, skateboarding, track, karate, or horseshoes—any athletic activity will do. By taking the lessons from the field to your personal and business arenas, you can win in the game of life.

EXERCISE

Fair Play

What difference does participating in sports make in your life in dealing with others? What teacher or coach brings out the best in you, and what qualities do they have that you admire? Write down what you have learned from any sport. Implement the lessons in your everyday encounters.

☆

"It's not whether you win or lose, it's how you play that counts. Care, share, and be fair."
Father Patrick McGrath

The Gift of SUCCESS

By Bernie Siegel, MD

One young man said to me, "My father ruined my life when I was eighteen. He gave me a million dollars and told me I had to be a success." What would his father have said if he started a charity with the money? What is success anyway?

I have witnessed the suffering of many children of millionaires whose parents gave them money to use to make more money to become a "success". These parents are giving their children mottoes to die by and not live by because money is not the only meaning of success.

What is your definition of success? If it is a big estate, a fancy car, and lots of dollars in your pockets, you will never be happy or successful. When speaking to a group of young millionaire business owners, I asked, "Is life fair?" They yelled "No" louder than any group I have ever spoken to. They didn't feel successful.

A very sad young man was in therapy because he was devastated that he was not a "success" according to his standards. One day a light bulb went on, and he exclaimed, "When you are a success you are not happy, but when you are happy you are a success." Bingo—happiness is success, not the other way around.

When we help others, it makes us happy. Decide how you want to serve the world, and then go do it. You will be living your life and accomplishing what we are all here to accomplish in our lifetimes. And when you enjoy serving in your own unique way, Monday morning will not be a threat to your health and you will never feel like you are working. It is only work if there is someplace else you'd rather be. Accept the fact that you are mortal and don't waste your time doing what you do not want to do or things you're not good at. Learn to say *no* to the world and *yes* to yourself.

When I was a child, my parents taught me that being happy was being successful. When a decision was to be made, there was only one way to decide: "Do what will make you happy without hurting anyone." When the inevitable troubles and difficulties occurred I heard; "God is redirecting you. Something good will come of this." And when material things and finances were involved, my parents would say "Money is to make life easier for people." I came from a minority group. I was loved by my parents, studied diligently, and got along with God.

Understand that a perfect world is an illusion and not a reality. What makes our love and actions meaningful is that we have a choice. Life is simply a school where we study how to live, laugh, and learn. There are no mistakes, just lessons to be learned. We were meant to be human beings and not human doings. Success is not determined by the money in your bank account, but by the love in your heart.

EXERCISE

Success Meter

Make a list of all the simple things you are capable of doing, for instance, tying your shoes, making a bed, tossing a salad, mowing the lawn, babysitting, etc. Then make a list of all of your positive actions and qualities: helping a friend, upbeat personality, caring heart. Every day add at least three items your lists and keep reviewing your lists until you do feel confident. Then pat yourself on the back, smile, and revel in your success! Never think of yourself as a failure.

☆

"Happiness is success.
A successful life is your choice."
Cynthia Brian

The Gift of SUPPORT

By Katie Kale

"Whatever you choose to do, we will support you!"

How much more fortunate could a girl be than to hear these words every day for the past seventeen years from the people who love her most—Mom and Dad! Yes, I am that lucky lady.

I am blessed to live in a community that is family-oriented and where parents are heavily involved in the activities of the children. My parents are my role models. Besides beating the odds with a twenty-year marriage, they both have successful careers they enjoy. The lesson they taught me is to follow my heart and be happy

My dream began at age five when I started dancing at a local studio. It progressed to making home movies, showcasing them at premieres in the neighborhood, and serving hot buttered popcorn. My folks were my biggest fans.

These small ovations gave me oodles of confidence that has served me well throughout my high school career. I served in leadership positions as a class president, cheerleading captain, chairperson of committees, and student body vice president, in addition to participating on several athletic teams. All the while, I have maintained a 4.0 average and had the satisfaction of working with underprivileged children in other communities.

This year I reached for the stars and decided to pursue my life long dream of becoming an actor. Again, my parents encouraged me. I was thrilled when I was cast in the lead role of a feature film on my very first audition. It's been a wild ride of booking numerous jobs, meeting incredibly creative people, and knowing that there is a big bright world to discover. I could have never accomplished my goals without the love and support of my family. Every time I felt discouraged, my mom would be there with a shoulder to cry on. After letting me wallow in my self-pity for a short time, she'd gently nudge me to try again. I always appreciate her advice.

No person is an island. To achieve our goals, we have to share our dreams and surround ourselves with people who believe in us. I found my team.

Thanks Mom, thanks Dad. I'll continue to make you proud!

EXERCISE

Support Your Team

It's so easy not to appreciate our parents during our teenage years. We tend to take them for granted and spend as little time as possible enjoying their company. This week invite your Mom or Dad or both to go to a coffee shop. Turn off your cell phone. Treat them to a favorite beverage. Ask how you can support them. Engage them in conversation and enjoy spending time with the people who gave you life. Go out of your way to express your appreciation and gratitude. Be part of the dream team!

☆

"Appreciate support from others
and offer it in return."
Katie Kale

The Gift of SURVIVAL

By Bernie Siegel, MD

What can teenagers do today to ensure a healthy future, emotionally, physically, and spiritually?

Studies reveal that when children grow up feeling loved by their parents, they have a greater opportunity to be well adjusted. When young people experience indifference or even abuse at the hands of those who are supposed to guide and care for them, they can end up confused, depressed, or angry. However, such a bad start can be overcome.

Teenagers can abandon their past with all the associated negativity and use their anger and energy to change their lives by *reparenting* themselves. A woman who was abused as a child stated, "When you let love into your prison, it can change all the negative experiences in your life and turn them into something meaningful." You can also look for substitute parents who will accept and love you even when they are critical of your actions. Find someone to coach you through life. People who have experienced a major loss or illness can be especially skilled. These individuals know how to heal from tragedy and what lessons are important for survival.

A young man I know, Tony Johnson, was planning to commit suicide. Tony was HIV positive due to sexual abuse inflicted upon him by his parents and others. I told him we could get a gun and kill his parents instead. He said, "No, I never want to be like them." He understood that the behavior of his parents had literally "killed" his will to live. Yet, revenge was not the answer. Through this he also accepted that suicide is never the treatment of choice. Life is a gift to treasure. He went on to write a book about his experiences, "A Rock and A Hard Place".

You are meant to love yourself and your neighbors. Do not eliminate your life. Eliminate the things in your life that are killing you physically, emotionally, and spiritually by sharing your pain and getting the assistance you need to move forward. Never give up the life you want for yourself to please others. Lose the untrue self and save your authentic life.

You are a divine child. Get your baby pictures out and live for that awesome child. To survive, find meaning in your life; express appropriate anger when you are not treated with respect; ask for help when you need it, and do not deny your needs and feelings Say no when necessary, find time to play, and savor your chocolate ice cream. Use your feelings to help protect you, and redirect your life rather than being disturbed by them or turning to drugs to numb you. Live an authentic life, and don't just play a role in someone else's movie. When you need attention or love, ask for it. Make noise, move, and express your feelings.

EXERCISE

Survival Kit

Tonight, think of who your role model is. Who would you like to be tomorrow morning when you wake up? Write down all the qualities and characteristics you wish you had. When you arise tomorrow, look at the list, and start acting and behaving like the person you wish to become. Your lifetime is what you are given to accomplish becoming who you were meant to be. We are all actors, so start now. The curtain is up.

☆

"Survive, thrive, and be alive."
Cynthia Brian

The Gift of TALK

By Cynthia Brian

"Way cool!" "So groovy!" "He is so hip!" "What's happening?" "That's bitchin'." "How neat!" "Foxy lady!" "Are you wired?" "That's totally wicked!" "Can you dig it?" "Right on! "Righteous!" "Funky!" "Dude!" "She's heavy!" "Cool cat!" "Let's hang!" "So busted!" "What a bummer!" "Totally!" "Yo!" "Far out!"

Do you recognize these slang slogans? Every teen generation creates it's own lingo. Are you having a gas? Made it to first base? Who bagged my wallet? I need some bread. He's an animal. Did your parents go ape? Don't have a cow if you don't know what I'm talking about!

Growing up as a teen in the flower-child generation of the 1960s and 1970s, I have always been fascinated by the language of the youth culture. Of course, in our day, we thought we were totally cool, hip, *avant-garde,* tight, and the first generation of teens that were in the groove. *Not!*

Throughout history young people have always created their own "argot" or "jargon", a specialized vocabulary or set of idioms used to keep adults from understanding their conversations. In today's technological revolution, an entirely new lingo has evolved. We all now talk about crackberries, googling, webisodes, vlogs, and wikidemia. Our text messages include BFF (best friends forever), IDK (I don't know), LOL (laughing out loud), OMG (oh my God!) ROFL (rolling on the floor laughing), and TMI (too much information).

Heather Brittany and I recently co-hosted an episode called "Decoding Teen Talk" on our nationally syndicated radio show, *Starstyle-Be the Star You Are!* Although barely out of her teens, Heather confessed that the newest profusion of idioms baffle even her. She shared her secret codes from her recent high school years. Texting the numbers 143 meant "I love you!"; 823 was "thinking of you"; and BRB was "be right back". Code nine was the signal that parents were around while PAW designated that parents are watching. Really! I was clueless.

By the time this book is published, these terms may be passé, but for now, learn the slang of the day.

Bling: jewelry
Tatted out: covered in tattoos
Cougar: older woman dating a younger man
Cupcaking: public display of affection

Flirtationship: prolonged flirtation with a friend not involving any physical contact
Frenemy: person close to you who hurts your feelings
Peeps: closest friends or family
Disco nap: a short sleep before clubbing
Check vitals: to monitor your emails, telephone, or any messages anywhere
Friend: used for connections on social networking sites
Jump the Shark: to have peaked and now be on a downward spiral
Rock: to manifest greatness
Talk Smack: to belittle a person
Fo' Shizzle: certainly cool
Obvi: obviously
Totes: totally
The Bomb: ultimate favorite
Tight: fantastic
Wack: unjustifiable
Nutter: a crazy person

Talk to your parents and grandparents to find out what the vernacular of their era was. Do some research on slang through the centuries. Check out old books, magazines, and films for examples. You'll have a great laugh as well as realize that even your elders were once young and probably unconventional.

If you want to be cool and in the groove, stop talking jive and slap me some skin because you are soooo sweet! Ten-four, good buddy. We'll be tripping, rock on! Cya later alligator. Peace. Badonkadonk. The end.

EXERCISE

Talk On!

What is a POW, PAD, PIG, or a PIMP? Write down the terms you are talking about right now! Are you tweeting, twisting, jabbing, and jiving? Let's roll! ☺ :-)

☆

"Look up, laugh loud, talk big, keep the color in your cheeks and the fire in your eye, adorn your person, maintain your health, your beauty and your animal spirits."
William Hazlitt 1778-1830, Essayist

The Gift of THANKSGIVING

By Heather Brittany

Something wonderful happened to me my freshman year of college. I didn't get to go home for Thanksgiving. Now, I know that does not exactly sound like great news at first, but it later turned out to be a beautiful blessing in disguise.

My class schedule for my freshman year was a full one with courses running from morning until evening five days a week. Unfortunately, there was no way I could go home to northern California from San Diego for the holiday because that Thursday was my only day off since I had an off-campus job on Friday and Saturday which was essential for my tuition. Not wanting to be alone on such an important family celebration, I asked the leader of an on-campus community service club to which I belonged if she knew of any shelters that needed help in their kitchens on Thanksgiving. She informed me that all of the soup kitchens were fully staffed with volunteers, but there was another option. A communal home for people suffering with AIDS was seeking volunteers to come and spend the day with the patients. Because of the stigma attached to this disease, it was difficult to attract helpers. To me, this sounded like the perfect opportunity.

At my apartment, I baked cookies, then set off early on Thanksgiving morning to spend time with these patients. As I drove the two hours to the location, my phone kept ringing with well wishes from my family and friends. Everyone was calling to say how much I was missed and to send me their love. Over and over I heard, "How we wish you were here with us, but you are always in our hearts!" This made my spirits soar, to know how much I really was cherished.

I arrived at my destination and was greeted by the nurses who provided an orientation to prepare me for what I might experience and see during the day. The men and women patients were quite sick and very gaunt. AIDS stands for Acquired Immune Deficiency Syndrome. It is a pandemic disease, which progressively reduces the effectiveness of the immune system, leaving individuals susceptible to multiple infections and tumors.

The day began with me in the kitchen preparing a traditional Thanksgiving feast with all the trimmings. Although my phone was switched to vibrate mode, it never stopped ringing with continued greetings from family. In the living room, I sparked conversations with several of the patients. One gentleman in particular caught my attention. Although he was terribly ill, he was filled with energy, excitement, and *joie de vivre.* He showed me a favorite book of his, a photographic history of Marilyn Monroe. Repeatedly, he thanked me for sharing the hours with them. "You see, we don't get many visitors here, " he said. At that moment, my phone vibrated again. My voice mail contained yet another message from my family who missed me. I realized that I had been here in this home with these special people all day and not once had a phone rung or any visitor stopped by to wish them a Happy Thanksgiving. I know they all have families somewhere, but somehow, they were alone today.

The hours chatting passed quickly, and, as evening progressed into nightfall, it was time to leave. I hugged each person goodbye and left for home. On the drive back, I realized how fortunate I was to have a family that missed me, treasured me, and wanted me with them. Moreover, I felt blessed that my class schedule conflicted with my homecoming because I was able to spend the day in a place so filled with love and gratitude. As thankful as they were for my presence, they were a gift to me. This was the most memorable Thanksgiving I have ever experienced, and for that I am so grateful.

America is a country of great abundance, yet, everyday most of us complain about the lack in our lives. Being human means that all of us, regardless of race, religion, economics, politics, or gender, will have difficult times and challenges to overcome. Take time to give thanks for the little things *every day,* not just once a year. Be grateful for what you have. When we are grateful, we are rewarded with a sense of honor and personal strength. Say "thank-you," for every gift you receive, positive or negative, because everything in life is a blessing. When things seem not to be going in the right direction, life may be giving you a lesson in appreciation. Gratitude exalts the heart and feeds the soul. Having an attitude of gratitude makes every moment shine brightly.

Everyday is Thanksgiving Day when you live, learn, laugh, and love in the moment.

EXERCISE

Give And You Shall Receive

Mark your calendar for a day of thanksgiving, and volunteer your time in a place that needs your presence. Consider places that most people ignore or forget—homes with AIDS sufferers, the elderly, the disabled, or those with dementia. It's as simple as going on-line to find an organization that needs your help in your locale. The more you give to others, the more you give to yourself. Have a great Thanksgiving any day of the year.

☆

"Thanksgiving is today.
Share the abundance."
Heather Brittany

The Gift of TIME

By "Action" Jack McClendon

"They've got too much free time" is what I would say to myself about people with ample leisure time. I had no time to chill. My daily routine was jammed. As a husband, active churchgoer, and fulltime student with a fulltime job, I had endless work to keep me wired. I felt like family and friends relied on me for everything. My fidgeting hands and legs hip-hopped like Lil' Wayne. I blamed my time crunch on everything and everyone but myself.

Then, one really stressed-out day I noticed a hard, marble-sized lump in my throat that looked like an extra Adam's apple. The doctors thought it was cancer and ordered me to get an MRI immediately. Fortunately, the tests revealed that my condition was result of stress—not cancer.

On the way home from the clinic I heard myself yell, "Help! Save me from myself!" I thought it was a funny thing to say—until I realized it was a wake-up call. I needed help to change the way I was using my time, but I wasn't sure why. Was I simply too busy? Was the clock to blame? Who was I kidding—I was responsible for my hamster-wheel lifestyle. I wondered how I could save myself from me.

Then I recalled reading that if you ask yourself an introspective question before going to sleep, your subconscious mind would answer it. So I softly repeated, "How can I use time more wisely?", until I slipped into sleep. That night I had a vivid dream that exceeded anything I could have imagined. Although the dream occurred over a dozen years ago, I remember it as if it were last night. I dreamt a step-by-step, detailed, workable time management system. It was like magic! I learned that the gift of time was connected to my ability to say "no" to good things and say "yes" to the best things. I discovered how to embrace prioritization.

My dream gave me insight and self-respect about my limitations. Applying the time management system that I developed has affected my life in countless positive ways. I discovered how to tap into my subconscious mind so that I can problem-solve even while sleeping. I've learn to adjust my working style from a multitasking mindset into a single-focus, problem-solving one.

Teen life can be filled with non-stop activity. Family obligations, the dating scene, and school deadlines can be overwhelming. That's why some teenagers turn to drugs which they think will help them keep up-with everything. But with the right time-management system, you'll avoid all of the snags that drugs and quick fixes create. And you'll discover how a balanced time-management system will help you defeat stress in the short and long-term. It will give you all the free time that you need to be at your best.

Today, I regularly block out free time everyday because I've learned that without free time I can never truly be free.

EXERCISE

Time Machine

Ask yourself an introspective question before going to sleep. Softly repeat the problem-solving question until you fall asleep. Keep a notepad near your bed and note how your subconscious mind directs you when you awake.

☆

"Seek free time because without it you can never be free; time is a gift to bless you—not to stress you."
Action Jack

The Gift of TODAY

By Cynthia Brian

Aunt Helen telephoned to tell me she had found a poem that had hung on her bedroom wall, inspiring her throughout her childhood. Reading it brought back memories of growing up poor, barefoot, and happy with her five siblings, including my mother, godmother, and my maternal grandparents, Nonie and Pa who had immigrated to California from Switzerland in the early part of the twentieth century. Even though it had been more than seven decades since she had read the poem, the impression these words imparted to her in her youth had created a lasting effect throughout her lifetime. "You know, Cynthia, when I read the poem again, it reminded me of you and what you teach in your seminars. I'd like to share it with you." I was eager to receive a copy.

A few days later, a manila envelope arrived in the mail. I gently opened the package and read Aunt Helen's endearing message which was paper clipped to the small, yellowed poster dated 1918. The title of the poem summed up the way I attempt to live my life each moment while encouraging my students, clients, family, and friends to do likewise. I would like to share this gift with you.

Live Life Today

Live life today as though today were all,
As thought this very morning you were born.
Your yesterdays are days beyond recall;
Tomorrow does not come until the morn.
Rest not upon the victories you have won;
Because you lost, surrender not to fear.
Your yesterday was ended with the sun.
Tomorrow has not come. Today is here.
Douglas Molloch

Almost a century after this poem was published, the message is more pertinent than ever. However, Aunt Helen was incorrect when she said that I have *always* lived for today. Actually, I learned to live each day to the fullest the hard way.

I was working on a movie in Hollywood, so I invited my youngest brother, David, to spend the week with me. David had been instrumental in getting me booked in commercials and films, and I was anxious to express my gratitude to him by showing him a great time. However, David was busy working on our ranch, plowing the vineyards, and said that he would come with me the following week because he wanted to finish his chores. While chatting, he told me he had "one more field to plow." I was disappointed and a bit angry that he couldn't come share the limelight with me now, but we agreed to meet within the next seven days.

He never did make it to the movie set. The day after our conversation, the tractor he was driving turned over. David died instantly. He was only sixteen.

Today is the only time we have. We can't turn back the clock or push "replay." There are no dress rehearsals, and this is not a test. We get one shot at hitting the right target. One shot! Today we have the opportunity to be the stars we were born to be.

When we are teenagers, we tend to think we are immortal and invincible. We're inclined to live for tomorrow. We can't wait to be old enough to get a driver's license, go on a date, experience a first kiss, have a weekend sleepover, get a job, or go to college. Sometimes we spend so much energy worrying about our mistakes of yesterday and pondering our tomorrows that we miss the fun and adventures in the present. When we embrace our past with love while forgiving the offenses and hurts, we can concentrate on living in the moment today and create a plan for tomorrow. Don't waste time with silly, unimportant grievances. Dream of your future, knowing that tomorrow never comes. There is always only today. Take charge now and enjoy every minute.

Don't let a tragedy teach you that this moment is the only moment you'll ever have. Savor it. Live it. Rejoice for it. Now.

EXERCISE

Live Like You're Dying

If you were told you only have thirty days to live, what would be the legacy you want to leave behind? In a journal, write down the answers to these questions. How would you spend the next 43,200 minutes, which total thirty days? Who would you want to be? What people would you want to spend time with? What would you want to do? What words of endearment and gratitude would you express to others?

What new food would you want to try? What music would you listen to? What places would you visit? Do you have any regrets? Ask yourself how you want to be remembered. Read your responses. Then live fully. Today is a gift. Today is here.

☆

"Yesterday is history,
tomorrow is a mystery.
Today is a gift.
That's why we call it the present."

The Gift of
TRADITION

By Cynthia Brian

"I can't believe you allowed her out of the house with that outfit, Mom!" howled my son. "Did I really wear my hair like that?" I shrieked as I doubled over in hysterics. "Dad, you really liked pink," teased our daughter. It was a chilly Christmas Eve as our family snuggled under blankets in front of the roaring fire, drinking hot chocolate while watching our home made videos dating from the 1980's. At our home, reviewing family videos on Christmas Eve is a cherished tradition, filled with laughter, memories, and endearing moments of growing up.

Traditions are the foundation of the family unit. The word *tradition* comes from the Latin *traditionem***,** which means, "handing over or passing on". There is a real reason for every season to celebrate family rituals. Passing on traditions give us a sense of belonging, a feeling of joy, something to look forward to. When we pass down traditions, we pass a bit of our spirit and our heritage to those we love.

Over the years we have accrued many customs for our clan. Christmas has always been a favorite season as it is for so many people around the world. Besides the tradition of lighting the advent candle every day, we celebrate with a brunch in San Francisco followed by a special surprise. The night before Christmas is our home movie extravaganza, beginning with attendance at Mass, then a seafood feast we all share in preparing. This year, our son drove to the coast to buy fresh crab and fish from the fishermen, our daughter whipped up the gingerbread, and I set a beautiful holiday table, while my husband chose the beverage treats. When the children were younger, they sang in the Christmas choir or participated in the pageant. Some years we wander the neighborhood with friends singing Christmas carols, always ending the celebration watching videos from years past, reminiscing, laughing, crying, and feeling a sense of togetherness.

No matter how old the children are, Santa always arrives by Christmas morning, strewing presents from the fireplace in the living room, winding through the hallways to the fireplace in the family room. Once in awhile, he leaves a note for a treasure hunt, sending the kids scurrying around the house, shed, yard, and barn hunting for their Christmas cache. In the afternoon, we go to the ranch where I was raised to continue the tradition of our extended family Christmas. Although my dad has died, my mother entertains four generations with her delicious cooking, over-the-top decorating, and down-home hospitality. We break out instruments for our motley country band, a cacophony of ear-splitting music with washboards, spoons, pots, pans, harmonicas, and good old-fashioned foot stomping. We're all rock stars for an hour of silliness. Outside, thousands of twinkling lights adorn every bush, tree, and plant as we herald the spell of good cheer. Everyone anticipates the excitement of these holidays, and, although our traditions are predictable there is usually something new and fresh for the way we live right now.

We started a birthday tradition known as "Mudder-Dudder Day", when my daughter, Heather, turned three, since that is how she pronounced "mother-daughter." It's a day of girlie pampering highlighted by facials, manicures, pedicures, lunch, and a movie. At Halloween, our family would always join three other families at a beautiful, secluded hideaway in the woods of Mt. St. Helena to carve pumpkins and trick or treat around the doors of a classic Victorian. During my kids' teen years, Halloween meant a big bonfire at the top of the driveway, roasting marshmallows and serving hot cider to the trick-or-treaters with hot mulled wine for the adults. New Year's brought us to the coast near Eureka where the same group of friends from Halloween regaled each other on a cattle ranch, riding horses on the beach and foraging for Portobello mushrooms. The Eggsciting Easter Petting Zoo was the emphasis of our springtime tradition as we amused the town folk with the antics of our goats, chickens, rabbits, geese, ducks, turkeys, and other barnyard critters.

Illuminate your days with your own personal traditions. It doesn't matter what you create, as long as you have occasions that are the hallmark of your family. Traditions stretch us, bind us, and offer a feeling that we truly belong to one another. Much of our divine destiny depends on the rituals and traditions we create in the circle of family. And it is always fun to remember the wild clothes, the big hair, and the pink shirts we boasted at a different time of our life.

EXERCISE

Tradition Transitions

If you don't already celebrate any special traditions, start today. It can be as simple as a Sunday Game Night where every member of the family participates in a board game with silly prizes for the winner. We used to have a Bingo night and let my Swiss-Italian Nonie win. Her award would be a roll of toilet paper, making her howl with laughter. Her joy was our joy. Ask your parents to dig out movies of when you were a baby. Relish that beautiful innocence that was you. You'll grow a fond bond with your folks and siblings, and you'll look forward to each special event. Try a new twist on a recipe together or express your thankfulness with a note of appreciation. Pass on your legacy to create your own personal good ole' days.

☆

"You are the reason for the season!
Celebrate and honor your traditions."
Cynthia Brian

The Gift of TRIUMPH

By Cynthia Brian

My daughter, Heather, has always loved water. By age three, she was the youngest member of a six-and-under swim team. She was a fish without fear. When the gun went off at her first swim meet, she belly-flopped into the pool and did three breaststrokes. Then she grabbed the ropes and waved to the crowd, a huge smile on her face. She did another three strokes, stopped, and waved. She continued like this the entire length of the pool. Of course, she finished last, but in triumph. The crowd *loved* her!

That day set the tone for the rest of her swimming career. She competed for more than a dozen years. She did it for the joy and the challenge, but she won innumerable honors and awards.

Another of Heather's competitions allowed *me* a major triumph. The year 1999 found Heather and me at the Miss California Pageant in Fresno, California. She had been named Miss Teenage Contra Costa County and was representing our county at the state level. I conducted a live radio broadcast with the current Miss California and several of the aspiring contestants, including other young teens vying for Miss Teenage California. Then, I settled down to relax and enjoy the pageant.

Heather appeared at my elbow, a stricken look on her face. In her hand was the audiotape she had carefully prepared, a compilation of music for her dance/gymnastic routine in the talent competition. "Guess what, Mom. They can only play music on CDs. No audio tapes allowed."

Audiotapes were still the norm in 1999. In fact, all the radio shows I produced were saved to audiotapes and DATs. Our station didn't even own a CD player or burner. Did the organizers have any idea where we could get a CD made from the tape at the last minute? "No," they said. As Heather dashed off to get ready, I went into action. I drove to every radio station in Fresno, asking if they could burn the music to a CD. None had the equipment. I was referred to various recording agencies, but all were closed. It was Saturday.

Praying as hard as I could, I was pulling out of a parking lot when I saw a van with the logo of a music production company and a phone number. Eureka! I immediately dialed the number on my cell phone. A real person answered, and I told him about my dilemma. "We can't help you," he said, "but I know who can.

Where are you?" And he gave me directions and even met me at my destination to make sure all went smoothly. Within thirty minutes, Heather's music was on a CD. I felt giddy with triumph, and even the production company was pleased that they had solved our predicament and saved Heather's act.

Heather didn't win the state pageant, but she gave an awesome performance and had the time of her life. That was her triumph. Getting a CD made in Fresno on a Saturday was mine. Fill your days with similar triumphs, big and small, and bask in your achievements.

EXERCISE

Cue the Trumpets

At the top of a page in your journal, write "Triumphs," and make a list. Maybe it's the first time you cooked a dinner that was edible or rode a skateboard or got applause for something. Maybe it's finishing a task you really hated or going out of your way to do a good deed for which you'll get no praise or credit.

Praise yourself. Hear a hundred silver trumpets saluting each of your triumphs, resounding for your ears alone. You'll soon notice how many great things you can accomplish.

Victorious people complete projects; losers never finish. Triumph is the knowledge that "if it is to be, it is up to me!" As an achiever, you create your own positive forecast.

☆

"You don't have to beat someone or something to be triumphant. Triumph is about meeting high personal standards and goals. You are a victor because you do and give your best, whatever the actual outcome."

Cynthia Brian

The Gift of TRUST

By Cynthia Brian

You know in your heart what's needed. If you want to be trusted you must be trustworthy and truthful. Trust is the reliance on the integrity, character, and intention of another person.

The other day while lecturing in another city I bumped into the father of a client I had coached when she was six. "How's your beautiful daughter?" I inquired. "Fourteen and trouble!" he answered with a deep frown. "We can't trust a word she says. She smokes pot, gets drunk at parties, and sneaks away at sleepovers. She is now under house arrest." I remembered the cherubic, bubbly blonde beauty as sweet, smiling, and singing.

Walt Disney once said: "We're sure of just one thing. Everyone in life was once a child." All adults, parents, teachers, and guardians, were teenagers too, although it may seem like the dark ages. Alcohol, drugs, sleepovers, risky behavior, cheating, and sexual experimentation are temptations of adolescence. It doesn't mean you have to go along with the crowd to have a good time. Parents want to trust their kids, and, in return, kids want to trust their parents. Teachers trust that you won't cheat on tests. Employers trust that you won't steal. Trust entails mutual respect.

If your dad said he'd be at your baseball came at 5 PM and never showed up, he has breached your trust. The next time he tells you he's coming, you may not be so sure. Your parents trust you until you prove them wrong. If you say you are going to John's house, but you go to Susan's party instead, trust is broken. Trust is a risky business because relationships depend on integrity and truth.

For the most part, parents don't instigate house rules as punishment, but as safety measures. As parents, our job is to help you grow up to be a healthy, happy, balanced citizen. Peer pressure often leads a good kid down the danger trail. In the case of the father above, he wasn't' angry with his daughter, just deeply disappointed. He felt his daughter had misplaced the trust the family had in her, and therefore she was grounded, under "house arrest" to protect her health and welfare. She may have fallen in with irresponsible friends, imitating and adopting their behavior to be considered cool. Our friends are always mirrors of ourselves.

There is only one route to trust. You must be truthful, straight forward, confidential, and honest. Those little white lies always come back to bite you in the butt. Deception, cheating, and dishonesty are the quickest course to ruining your credibility and reputation. Talk to your parents as well as your friends. Trust is not to be assumed or presumed. You'll find in life there are many untrustworthy people that you'll want to distance yourself from, ignore, and not associate with. You don't want to be considered one of them.

EXERCISE

Trust Me

Speak the truth, the whole truth, and nothing but the truth. Honesty is always the best policy. Follow your sincere words with respectable actions.

☆

"Trust is earned, not given freely.
To be trusted, you must be trustworthy."
Cynthia Brian

The Gift of UNDERSTANDING

By Nora Catherine Nordan

I have kept all my diaries from my teenage years because I swore to myself that I would never let myself forget how terrible those years were. When my children become teenagers, I thought, I'll understand everything they're going through, and they'll be amazed at what a wonderfully perceptive mother they have. Like, how could she possibly know all this?

I must have been a terrible teenager. I didn't know what was going on inside me. I'd wake up in the morning full of the joys of life. The birds would be singing and life was wonderful. By the time I got home from school at 4 PM, the world had turned black, there was a thundercloud over my head, nobody understood me, nobody loved me, and I wished I were dead. My schoolbag got flung into a corner of the kitchen as I raced past Mum, slamming the doors as hard as I could on the way, until I reached the sanctuary of my bedroom. I hurled myself on the bed and wept copious tears. I was the unhappiest girl in the world. I just couldn't understand what was going on. From being a polite, bookish child, at about noon, I turned into a raging, moody, unpredictable termagant, a phase that was to last almost seven years. At around nineteen, I began to calm down, though there were still outbursts, particularly at my poor Mum, until I was way past twenty-one. If during one of my dramatic, locked-in-the bedroom, misery sessions, my mother ventured upstairs to try to find out what was wrong, I would let fly verbally and blame her for all the ills of the world—and my own. My mother being young herself—only thirty-four when puberty hit her eldest daughter—fired back, and we had some very heated arguments, to put it mildly, in every room of the house! My father, the respected family doctor, whose surgery was beside the family room, had frequently to emerge from the other side of the double, supposedly sound-proofed, door to try to pour oil on the troubled waters being navigated by the females in his life. I would get a stern reprimand and a reminder that, as *paterfamilias*, he expected me to show respect to my mother. "She is *my* wife…" What the patient waiting on the other side of the door must have thought of our domestic hiatus, I shudder to think.

Of course, now I realize what was going on—hormones. Way back in the sixties, we hadn't heard of hormones or PMT. Our home must have been a hotbed of hormones—my mother's and mine—ricocheting between the walls and around the corners. Duck, or you'll be hit! It wasn't even as if you could predict when the storms would blow in—even had we known of PMT it wouldn't have helped *us.* I have heard of families where females living in close proximity develop a kind of harmony in the timing of their menstrual cycles—my mother and I unfortunately remained irregular all of the years we spent under the same roof!

So when I in my turn had children, I dreaded their puberty, the door slamming, the yelling, the "nobody-understands-me-I'm-the-unhappiest-person-in the-world-I-wish-I-was-dead"...

However, I had sons, not daughters. As toddlers, one was the sunniest, most extroverted, even-tempered, and friendly child you could imagine. The other was silent and extremely strong-willed, with temper tantrums that could last for almost a whole day, leaving me, his poor mother, exhausted. I began to think "If he's like this now, what'll he be like as a teen? I'm so glad I kept my old diaries—I'll surely need them". But another, older, mother with grown-up children told me, "If he's like that when he's a toddler, you'll have no trouble when he's a teenager". So then I thought, "Oh, maybe the other one will be the teenage terror then. I'm glad I've still got my diaries!"

But what do you know, both my boys sailed through puberty with never a cross word, no doors slammed, no never-ending arguments. They were the nicest, politest, most well balanced teens you could ever hope to meet. So I never needed those diaries after all, and to this day my sons have no idea what a horrible teen their mother was!

I guess the moral of this story is—there's hope for teens and their mothers, and we all survive somehow. And some of us parents of teens even get to draw on our hard-earned wisdom—and some of us never need to. You just never know until it's your turn, do you?

Being a teenager had its wonderful moments, and it can really be dreary at times. It may be hard to believe, but there is light at the end of the tunnel. Once you're through your teen years, you'll be a better and wiser and more mature person. You will have achieved a greater understanding of yourself and what motivates you, cheers you, and upsets you. You will have gained insight into how others feel and how you make them react, and how and why they react to you. The teenage years are valuable preparation for your adult years and for the relationships you will form with other people!

EXERCISE

Understanding Yourself and Others

★ If you've been keeping a journal as suggested, open your journal now to a blank page. Or buy yourself a nice blank notebook (or one with lines if your writing is wobbly). Or even open a file on your PC. Every day if you get the chance, or at least once a week, keep a journal of your feelings and emotions. Describe what made you feel super happy and glad to be a teen, and describe what put you down in the dumps. Try to see if you can find a pattern—when did you feel good, and when did you feel unhappy? What caused these emotions? See if you can find strategies that help you avoid the people and places that cause the negative influences.

★ Log on to a biorhythm calculator. It can help you plan your life. Some people find it very helpful to calculate their physical, emotional, and intellectual biorhythms for a month at a time. That way they'll know when they're going to have super days when they feel they can conquer the world, or days when it would be better to stay quietly in a corner and let the world go by. If you spot a so-called "triple negative day" coming up, for example, it might be best to avoid any situation that could get you into an argument with your Mom or Dad.

★ You could even plot your parents' biorhythms. You'll know when Mom or Dad is having an "off" day, and confrontations are best avoided. Or you can spot that golden opportunity to approach them for an increase in your allowance. Parents are human too. Like children, they blossom when they receive positive feedback and approval from those they love.

★ Show your parents that you respect them, love them, and appreciate them, in spite of everything. Practice holding your tongue and keeping your temper at least one day a week.

☆

"If you want others to understand you,
you'll have to understand yourself first."
Nora Catherine Nordan

The Gift of UNIQUENESS

By Allyn Evans

Relever means to lift up, to rise," Jodi Shilling said of the name she chose for her studio. It also means to take down, record, react, respond, plot, or spice. "It explains my story. Many times throughout my life, I've felt pushed down. I was told I couldn't accomplish what I set out to do. I was told I needed to change everything about myself, and I believed it."

Jodi grew up in small-town Indiana, and when she was young, her farmer father had a hard time making ends meet. "We didn't have much money, and I had to wear the same clothes over and over. I was the child with the cooties, the one the other kids called Groddy Jodi." Add to that excessive shyness and an almost crippling tendency to perfectionism. If she couldn't do something perfectly, she didn't want to do it at all. Jodi consistently scored in the lower levels in reading and math. Then there was her lisp and funny voice. "All these things added up," she said. "I was hard to understand, which fed my insecurities."

By middle school, Jodi she had conquered most of her perfectionism tendency by emphasizing her positive attributes and not dwelling on her weaknesses. With hard work, her grades soared. Her parents' finances improved, and she enrolled in dancing and singing lessons to help her overcome her shyness. She loved performing arts and continued them throughout high school.

Jo Rowan, founder of the Dance Department at Oklahoma City University, saw Jodi perform and encouraged her to audition for Rowan's program. Jodi was able to get a scholarship. After awhile, Jodi wanted something more. "It's about the journey and not about the end results," Rowan told Jodi. "If you're not happy with the journey, you shouldn't be doing this."

Jodi created a furor when she signed up for acting lessons her junior year. She didn't know students weren't allowed to enroll in the dance and acting programs at the same time. "I wanted to take a few acting classes," she said. Even though it caused problems, the dean of the theatre department gave her his support, and Jodi discovered what she really wanted to do.

But her teacher hated her speaking voice, and told her she would never make it in acting. Falling back on her dancing abilities, she auditioned for the chorus in the musical, *Chicago*, for the summer stock program. "I blew the dance audition," she confessed. "Afterward I decided to make a joke. They laughed, and I decided to tell a few more. They kept laughing. By the end of the day, I had been invited to play the lead!"

Jodi headed to New York City to pursue her Broadway dream. Acting coach after acting coach told her she needed to change her voice. "I hired a speech therapist and voice coach. Both tried to teach me to talk in a lower register. It didn't work." She then hired a career coach who tried to change everything else about her. "When my money ran out, I finally had to stop. I had worked so hard and paid people lots of money. What a waste."

That's when she finally started thinking about her strengths. "I was trying so hard to be someone I wasn't. No one was hiring me." She decided if she sounded like a cartoon character, then maybe she'd have more success on TV. She auditioned for a Los Angeles agent. "You're unique," the agent told her. "You're special." Jodi left New York for Los Angeles and never looked back. Her original mentor, Jo Rowan, had been right. Finding her path had been about enjoying the journey.

Jodi found that the more she accepted herself and build on her strengths, the more work she got. "The most valuable lesson I learned," says Jodi, "and will never forget, is you need to be who you are. Be yourself because that's the best self you can be. That's the self who will get you work. That's the self who will open doors. That's the self who will rise to the top! That's the self who will relevé."

EXERCISE

Rise Up and Be Yourself

Take a moment to evaluate your talents and strengths. If you can't think of anything unique about yourself, ask someone close to you, like your mom or best friend, to help. Write down your gifts and pledge to cultivate your uniqueness. You can do this by taking a class or joining a club of people with a similar interest.

☆

"The most valuable lesson I learned, and will never forget, is you need to be who you are."
Jodi Shilling, actress

The Gift of
VOLUNTEERISM

By Elyse Kolnolski

It is surprising that I enjoy volunteering so much because my first volunteer job was actually a punishment from my parents. Little did they know that it would lead me to find a new hobby that I really enjoyed and continue today, even though that punishment has long been completed.

Volunteering lifts my moods because I know that I have helped someone else. One of the most memorable places I have volunteered was an assisted-living facility. I was assigned to be the Bingo caller and to lead the weekly craft project. Bingo was easy and I was a brilliant caller. Then it was time for our craft project. Our assignment for the week was to create a mock stained-glass box using tissue paper plus a cornstarch and water mixture.

The elderly participants and I were having a great time, talking, laughing, and enjoying one another's company. I was having difficulty making my box because sticky globs of mashed up tissue paper coated my fingertips and my hands kept fusing together.

Two of the participants, Janis and Frank, were especially amused at my inability to fashion a container. Their boxes were beautiful, as were everyone else's. What was my problem? They encouraged me to keep at it, but I was still quite embarrassed. I was supposed to be the leader of the craft project, yet I was the only one having trouble.

Frank examined the box of "cornstarch" that I had been using in my mixture. He looked at it, then looked at me, and burst out laughing. I couldn't figure out what was so funny, but Janis also burst into giggles when Frank showed her the box.

"Sweetie, this isn't cornstarch," Janis managed to say between gasps of glee. "It's the fast-drying, super-adhesive we use for fixing ceramic figurines." "You're pasting your fingers together. That's why you're having so much trouble," Frank explained.

I looked at both of them, then at the box in stunned disbelief. I cracked up. What an idiot I was not to have noticed. They started laughing again, and their joy at my blunder made the day so worthwhile. The following week before the craft period started, they came up to thank me for the fun of the previous week. Frank and Janis explained that, before my arrival, both of them had been going through some challenging, unhappy days. My little goof had lifted their spirits and provided entertainment. Their response taught me that laughing at our mistakes could make a big difference. I thought I had volunteered to assist the elderly, but they were the ones who assisted *me*, teaching me to roll with the punches and not take myself so seriously.

Volunteering is like giving away a piece of yourself, only to have it returned to you in an even better condition and twice as valuable as it was originally. Volunteering gives you a feeling of peace, and makes you smile. Volunteering brightens everything you do, giving you the opportunity to change people's lives, especially your own. It's also a great way to meet people, make new friends, and be exposed to different aspects of life. When we help others, we feel really great about ourselves.

How do you find what is the best volunteer position for you? Ask yourself what it is that you really enjoy. If you like reading, creating crafts, playing with kids, rescuing animals, building houses, delivering meals, raising money for cancer research, feeding the homeless, or even working on a political campaign, there is a non profit organization or charity who will welcome your involvement. The possibilities are endless.

Volunteering is also a great way to learn new skills. It's like taking a course for free or trying out a job before deciding a career path. Volunteering also helps us forget about our own problems for a while and focuses our attention on making a difference in the world.

Find an organization you believe in. When you like the work and the organization likes you, you'll have a good match. An incredible growing experience awaits you. Enjoy.

EXERCISE

Making a Difference

How do you find volunteer opportunities? Visit the career center at school and check for openings. Advisors are always happy to help you find an appropriate cause. Or go on-line and use a free service like VolunteerMatch.com, which is what I did. When you contact the charity, ask for the volunteer coordinator. Be prepared to tell him or her about yourself. Here are a few questions that are usually asked:

- ★ What do you know about our organization and our mission?
- ★ Why do you want to volunteer?

- What are your special skills?
- How do you think you can serve?
- How many hours are you willing to volunteer?
- Do you have transportation?
- What are your interests and why have you chosen our charity?

You also may ask them questions about their expectations and explain how you hope to benefit from the experience. If you feel you have a good fit with the organization, start volunteering. There may be a learning curve, so make sure to show up several times before trying a different organization.

Many schools today require a certain number of community service hours before you graduate. Volunteering teaches responsibility, looks great on your college applications, and is impressive for job interviews. Most of all, you will have the satisfaction of knowing that you are doing your part to give back to your community.

☆

"The paradox of life is that the more we serve others, the more we serve ourselves."
Cynthia Brian

The Gift of WRITING

By Dallas Woodburn

My computer screensaver is a photograph of a six-year-old girl perched at the kitchen table in front of an old-fashioned manual typewriter. She sits up on her knees to be tall enough to reach the keys, and stares intently at the blank piece of paper in front of her, oblivious to everything save for the story unfolding inside her mind.

I am that little girl, now grown into a young woman of twenty-one. My screensaver captures the essence of who I am: a dreamer, a creator, a storyteller trying to share with others the magic I've discovered in my own imagination. To say it plainly, I am a writer.

I was ten years old when I published my first book. Now, more than a decade later, I'm still reaping the benefits of the gift of writing: self-confidence, a means to express myself, and hopefully a path to change the world for the better in some small way.

How did my journey begin? With one little idea—and a little naiveté, too. In fifth grade, I applied for and received a $100 school grant to write and self-publish a children's book of short stories and poems that I called *There's a Huge Pimple On My Nose*.

One of the perks to publishing a book at such a young age is that I didn't understand how difficult the project should be. I plunged into the writing world with excitement instead of fear. Furthermore, I used my young age as an advantage when marketing my book. "What better way to promote youth literacy," I wrote in my cover letters, "than a book written for kids by a kid?" I bravely sent out my book everywhere I could imagine, and scored reviews in not only my local Ventura, California newspaper, but also in the national magazines *Girl's Life* and *CosmoGirl*. A book review in *The Los Angeles Times* praised: "If you simply want some remarkable writing, it would be hard to find a book more satisfying."

I began speaking to schools and youth groups about my publication journey and was moved by the positive and enthusiastic response I received. Many kids tell me they did not think they could be writers, but after hearing my talk they are inspired to write stories of their own.

Motivated to reach as many kids as possible, in 2000 I founded a nonprofit organization "Write On!" to encourage kids to discover joy, confidence, and a means of self-expression through reading and writing. I have personally found during my time spent tutoring kids, including mentally challenged students, that keeping a journal often increases self-esteem and opens the lines of communication with others. In seven years, "Write On!" has donated 10,140 new books (worth approximately $70,000) to underprivileged kids, whose smiles buoy my spirits through any writer's block, rejection, or weariness I face the rest of the year. I have been told that for many of the recipients of my annual Holiday Book Drive, these books are the only Christmas gifts they receive.

As legendary basketball coach John Wooden says, "You'll never succeed if you're afraid to fail." So take chances. Be bold, because opportunities have a way of snowballing to create more opportunities. Turn "disadvantages" into advantages. Above all else, approach your life with wide-eyed excitement, enthusiasm, and passion!

EXERCISE

Write On!

Grab a blank piece of paper, or open a blank document on your computer, and visualize a place. Close your eyes and imagine you are there. Sit there for a minute or two just thinking about this place. What does it look like? Smell like? Feel like? Sound like? What emotions do you associate with this place? Memories? Desires? Fears?

Now, open your eyes and face the blank page with a fresh mindset. Look at the clock, and give yourself five minutes. Ready, set, go! Now write. For the next five minutes, don't let your pen leave the paper, or your fingers leave the computer keys. Just write. No judgments, no inhibitions. Don't limit yourself. Don't think too much. Just write. It doesn't matter if there are misspellings or grammar mistakes. It doesn't matter if things don't exactly follow or don't quite make sense. That can all be fixed later. For now, just write. Write a letter to your future self, predicting where you will be in five, ten, or even twenty years. What will you be doing, thinking, dreaming?

Hopefully once you get in the groove you'll fly past those five minutes and continue to write up a storm.

☆

"Infinitely more important than sharing one's material wealth is sharing the wealth of ourselves—our time and energy, our passion, and commitment, and, above all, our love."
William E. Simon,
former Secretary of the Treasury

The Gift of YOU

By T. L. Cooper

When I was fifteen, my English teacher assigned an essay called "If I Could Be Anyone in the World, I Would Be __________." The idea was for each of us to find a hero and identify why we admired that person.

I couldn't write it.

Every attempt I made felt false—like I was lying. I began to panic as the deadline neared because all I'd written was the title complete with the blank spot.

I read it aloud and finished the sentence with something that surprised me. "If I could be anyone in the world, I would be *me*!" Wow! Where did that come from? What was wrong with me? Did I really think that I was that special? I hoped writing the essay that way would propel me to identify a "hero," so I could write what was expected. Failure wasn't an option. Disappointing my parents—or myself—with a bad grade was unacceptable. In the end, I wrote an essay about what I liked about myself while acknowledging there were things I would like to change.

As I listened to my classmates read about how they wanted to be various famous football, baseball, or basketball players or that week's celebrity in the news, I became increasingly nervous. I hadn't identified a single "rich, successful" person I wanted to be.

Finally, it was my turn. I stood up and read the title. I paused at the end and glanced around the room. There were a few chuckles, more than one classmate made a face at me, and several expressions clearly said, "Why would she want to be herself?" I glanced at the teacher. Her expression screamed that she thought I'd copped out on the assignment. I turned my eyes back to my classmates. My eyes settled on one pair of eyes that stared back at me with interest—the eyes of a boy who made no secret he didn't like me.

I squared my shoulders and began to read about why I wanted to be myself. Before I finished the first paragraph, everyone was paying attention. I don't remember exactly what was in the essay, but it was my truth at the time. I talked about what I liked about myself, things I hoped to accomplish, and a few things I wanted to change about myself. I ended it by focusing on the fact that there was only one me, and if I wasn't me, I wouldn't exist. I'm not sure what words I used, but that was the idea. I wish I still had that essay…

After class, the boy who didn't like me stopped me as I left the room. He looked me straight in the eye and said, "That was brave. Maybe you're all right after all."

I earned an "A" on the assignment.

Knowing in my core that I like who I am and I have the power to change anything I don't like about myself has served me well when I faced challenges or celebrated victories throughout life. I've been able to hold my head high when other people didn't agree with my decisions. I've been able to encourage myself when the odds were against me. I've been able to ground myself when my ego was overfed.

Admiring others can be a starting point for people to change something they don't like about themselves, but accepting who you are is even more important. Only when you learn to accept yourself can you use what you admire in others to change your life and use others' successes or failures for your personal betterment.

EXERCISE

Accept Yourself

- ★ Answer the question "Would you rather be someone other than yourself?"
- ★ If yes, who? More importantly why?
- ★ If no, what makes you happy to be you?
- ★ Write down three things that would make you happier to be you. List three things for each that you can do to accomplish those things.

☆

"Love who you are and you'll be the best you possible!"
T. L. Cooper

AFTERWORD

Together we have completed our journey through ***Be the Star You Are! for TEENS***. I hope you have enjoyed the stories, lessons, exercises, and quotes and will incorporate some of the novel ideas into your daily life. Be advised that you still have a long road ahead filled with chills, thrills, triumphs, and tumbles. Look forward to each day as an unexpected gift that you get to unwrap and discover.

Cherish the past, dream of the future, and celebrate every moment of the present day. Always remember that you are unique and a special individual with talents, abilities, passions, skills, insights, and information that sets you apart. Use the gifts you've been given and the tools you've acquired to be the magnificent person you were born to be.

Do not allow the color of your skin, the nation of your birth, the religion you embrace, the social, economic, or political background of your family, your sexual orientation, or your physical disabilities halt or delay your progress. You are the captain of your ship. You and only you will determine whether you sail or sink in life. Live in no one's shadow. Live no one else's dream. Create a life and livelihood that you design.

You have permission to be an original. The world is ready for all of you. Show up and be counted. Allow your power to live, love, laugh, learn, and lead flow through you. It's that simple. Go on.

Don't forget the tools of being the star you are.

1. You must smile.
2. You must have fun.
3. You must be willing to be wild and wacky!

Grab this opportunity to experience your authenticity and the joyfulness of being. Keep this book in your backpack, your handbag, your car, or by your night stand. Open it daily for a quick pick-me-up and refresher course. Share ***Be the Star You Are! for TEENS*** with your friends, siblings, parents, teachers, coaches, and others. Anyone who interacts with adolescents will benefit from its contents. They'll probably want their own copy so give them the gift of growing.

If you have stories you'd like to communicate, please contact me, as my virtual door is always open.

Keep daring, keep caring
Keep moving, improving
Keep giving, keep living]
You are the star!

Life is a party and you are the greatest gift! Come on in and celebrate!

Thanks for being you!

Cynthia Brian

☆

Starstyle® Productions, llc
PO Box 422
Moraga, California 94556
www.cynthiabrian.com
Cynthia@bethestaryoaure.org
925-377-STAR

THEME SONG
BE THE STAR YOU ARE!

Words and Music by Frankie Laine and Deanne Hawley
Performed by Frankie Laine

Be the Star you are
Light the flame that burns
Deep within you heart
Where the real you yearns
To spread wings and fly.
Though the journey's long.
Keep love alive
And your spirit strong.
You're a seeker, a dreamer
With courage to give
Every precious part of you.
You're an artist, a poet
Who will never give up
'Till your dreams come true!
Let go of your fears.
You've traveled much too far.
Show the world your smile.
Be the Star you are.
Be the Star you are.
Be the Star you are.

"The End is your Beginning!" Cynthia Brian

MEET THE CONTRIBUTORS

Heather Brittany-Dating; Financial Literacy; Love; Sexuality; Thanksgiving

Heather Brittany, a former Outstanding Teenager of Contra Costa County and contestant for Miss Teen California, majored in Communications, English, and Women's Studies at San Diego State University. She has been acting and modeling since she was three days olds and was honored as the National Young Achiever of the Year. Heather is the youth co-founder of Be the Star You Are! charity and is the producer and co-host of the T42 segment on the nationally syndicated radio show, Starstyle-Be the Star You Are!. She is the creator of The Karmony Kollection™ for women—beautiful handmade clutches, canvases, and candles, using recycled and vintage materials. Through her employment as a Reproductive Health Assistant, Heather is dedicated to helping others make informed choices. She also volunteers her expertise with various non-profits. www.heatherbrittany.com; www.myspace.com/karmonyklutches.

Bud Bilanich-Optimism

Bud Bilanich, The Common Sense Guy, is an executive coach, motivational speaker, author, and blogger. Dr. Bilanich is Harvard-educated, but has a no nonsense approach to his work which goes back to his roots in the steel country of western Pennsylvania. Bud is a cancer survivor and lives in Denver with his wife Cathy. He is a retired rugby player and an avid cyclist. He likes movies, live theatre, and crime fiction. www.BudBilanich.com.

Ivan Burnell-Positivity

Ivan Burnell has been inspiring people to achieve more than they ever dreamed possible for the past thirty years. He has compiled his experiences into a set of courses called the YES Program that has helped thousands of people around the world make their lives happier and more fulfilled. Ivan is the author of *Living in the Unlimited Universe, Power of Positive Doing, Road to a Happier Marriage, Say YES to Life*. www.yesfactor.com.

Jill Byington-Laughter

Jill Byington has been writing and teaching for the past thirty years. She grew up in Washington State with two brothers, two sisters, two parents, and one bathroom. She still lives in the same area, but now she has one husband, one son, and three bathrooms. www.bethestaryouare.com.

Kim Carlson-Attitude

Wife, mother, first-time grandma, accountant, webmaster for Be the Star You Are!, trail-work volunteer, gourmet chef, designated family sommelier, carpenter, remodeler, landscaper, primitive camper, backpacker, and more, if Kim Carlson doesn't know how to do something, she will figure it out, and do it quickly, and with a great attitude.www.accountech.com.

Shirley Cheng-Challenges

Shirley Cheng (b. 1983) is a blind and physically-disabled, award-winning author (with twenty awards, including five Parent to Parent Adding Wisdom Awards), motivational speaker, self-empowerment expert, poet, author of nine books (including *Embrace Ultra-Ability!*) and contributor to fifteen books, and advocate of parental rights in children's medical care. Shirley is the recipient of numerous awards and won first prize in the 2005 national Be the Star You Are! essay contest. Visit www.ShirleyCheng.com.

C. Hope Clark-Hope

C. Hope Clark founded FundsforWriters.com, a reference enabling over 20,000 writers around the globe to improve their craft. She publishes in *Writer's Digest, The Writer Magazine*, and numerous magazines and online sites. She lives on the bank of Lake Murray in South Carolina and writes mystery novels for fun. www.fundsforwriters.com.

T.L. Cooper-You

T. L. Cooper grew up in Tollesboro, Kentucky. She graduated from Eastern Kentucky University where she studied Corrections and Juvenile Services. Her poetry, short stories, and articles have appeared in magazines and books. She is the author of the novel, *All She Ever Wanted*, and tied for first prize in the 2008 national Be the Star You Are! essay contest. She and her husband live in Oregon. www.tlcooper.com.

Maggie DiGiovannie-Responsibility

Maggie DiGiovanni, wife, mother, and author of the children's book, *Henley, the Frozen Hedgehog*. She is currently working on a children's novel, *Good Boy, Little Guy, and Old Man*, a story of a Scottish terrier, a Shih Tzu, and an ancient cat that protect the citizens of Sarasota, Florida. Maggie was the first prize winner in 2004 and tied for first in 2008 in the national Be the Star You Are! essay contest. www.freewebs.com/thewriterspad/.

Billijo Doll-Adventure; Encouragement

BilliJo Doll is a young adult author whose personal ministry is to help people of all ages become productive, positive, and passionate. Growing up on a ranch, BilliJo knows that when you get bucked off, you have to get back on the horse and ride. So goes life. Billijo is the host of the radio program, *Coping with Life*. www.billijodoll.com.

Allyn Evans-Uniqueness

Allyn Evans is the author of *Grab the Queen Power* as well as the *Living Happily Ever After with Your Daughter.* Allyn is a professional speaker on teens/tweens, a paid consultant, and presenter. Allyn's *The Alert Parent* is a weekly publication and runs in newspapers and magazines. www.allynevans.com, Jodi Shilling has appeared on *That's So Raven, Hannah Montana, Laughs for Life, and All My Children.* She's also starred in a Disney movie, *Raven's Makeover Madness* and other independent movie roles. www.jodishilling.com.

Sally Franz-Curiosity

Sally Franz is an author, an artist, a motivational speaker, a stand-up comedian, an inventor, and a grandmother. She has worked for Save the Children and UNICEF and is a staunch supporter of rights for women and children worldwide. 'Curiosity' is based on her upcoming book, *Scrambled Leggs.* www.Sallyfranz.com.

Rena Wilson Fox-Gratitude

Rena Wilson Fox is the mother of two wonderful children, a teenage girl and an eight-year-old boy. She is the owner and acquisitions editor of the company, *UnTapped Talent,* a book publishing company seeking the unpublished author with remarkable talent. www.UnT2.com.

James Christopher Gill-Adapting; Choice

James Gill has lived in the East Bay Area of northern California most of his life although originally born in Maryland. He loves to travel, has visited most of the United States, as well as several countries in Europe. He has one Bachelor's degree in Business Administration from Cal Poly University, and is pursuing a second Bachelor's in Computer Science at the University of California, Santa Cruz. James is the IT volunteer at Be the Star You Are! www.bethestaryouare.org.

Libby Gill-Risk

Proud mom Libby Gill headed PR at Universal, Sony, and Turner Broadcasting, and was the branding brain behind the launch of the *Dr. Phil Show.* Now an executive coach, speaker, and bestselling author, she's appeared on the Today Show, CNN, Oprah & Friends, and more. www.LibbyGill.com.

Joel Goodman-Humor

Dr. Joel Goodman is the founder of The Humor Project, Inc. (www.HumorProject.com), the first organization in the world to focus "fool-time" on the positive power of humor. Author of eight books and speaker to three million people on all seven continents, including Antarctica, Joel's goal is to help people get more smileage out of life. Joel@HumorProject.com, www.HumorProject.com.

Rachel Glass-Daring

Rachel Glass is a fifteen-year old high school sophomore living in the San Francisco Bay Area. Her life centers around close relationships with family and friends who have influenced her to be the best she can be and to shoot for the stars. Rachel loves to write because it helps her express her feelings. Her goal is to help others and be beneficial in this world. Rachel is a volunteer with Be the Star You Are! charity. www.bethestaryouare.org.

TJ Hoisington-Possibility

TJ Hoisington is the author of the international bestselling books, *If You Think, You Can! Thirteen Laws that Govern the Performance of High Achievers* and *If You Think You Can for Teens*. Co-author of *The Secret of the Slight Edge,* he speaks to audiences all over the world about Personal Development, High Achievement, Leadership, and Selling. www.greatnesswithin.com.

Katie Kale-Support

Katie Kale has been dancing and performing since age five. In high school, she maintained a 4.0 average while being active as student body vice president, cheer captain, and short stop on the softball team. Voted Most Spirited, she began her professional acting career at sixteen under the coaching guidance of Cynthia Brian, landing a lead role in a feature film on her first audition. Watch for Katie Kale at a theatre near you! www.bethestaryouare.com.

Elyse Kolnowski-Volunteerism

A seventeen-year old bookworm, Elyse Kolnowski loves books and reading. Like any typical 'word nerd' the public library is like a second home to her. A loving family adopted her when she was six and encouraged to volunteer with organizations. Elyse is a volunteer book reviewer and Teen Chairperson with the Star Teen Book Review Team at Be the Star You Are! www.bethestaryouare.org.

Pamela Lewis-Sleep

Pamela A. Lewis was born in 1953 in Jamaica, Queens, New York, the only child of British Guyanese immigrants. She attended public schools until she auditioned and was accepted to the High School of Music and Art. Her love of French won out over that of music, and she attended New York University where she majored in French Literature and holds both B.A. and M.A. degrees. She has been a French teacher for over twenty years, and teaches in a high school in Manhattan. She won Honorable Mention in the national Be the Star You Are! essay contest. Pamela still resides in Queens. plewis@hccs.hunter.cuny.edu.

Davis Lunsford-Affirmation; Now

Davis Lunsford, a seventeen-year-old writer, lives in Graham, Texas. Because of his Christianity, Davis has enjoyed writing about the character values espoused in ***Be the Star You Are! For Teens.*** A home-schooled student, he enjoys golf, water sports, Boy Scouts, 4-H, playing the bagpipes, and spending time with family. He was awarded Honorable Mention for his stirring essay in the national Be the Star You Are! essay contest. www.bethestaryouare.org.

Dr. Don Martin-Education

With nearly thirty years experience in Enrollment and Student Services, Dr. Donald C. Martin has counseled and consoled thousands of undergraduate and graduate school applicants and students at some of the nation's leading institutions, including Teachers College at Columbia University, the Graduate School of Business at University of Chicago, and the Medill School of Journalism at Northwestern University. His book, *Road Map for Graduate Study*, the first comprehensive book on the graduate school experience, educates and enlightens individuals, not only on how to successfully apply and get into the institution of their choice, but to understand how to get the most out of their student experience. www.gradschoolroadmap.com.

Jack McClendon-Time

Jack McClendon, former award-winning, syndicated talk-radio host, and columnist for Copley News, author of The Time Genie–Magical Essentials for Creating More Personal Time, is a labor and management representative with more than thirty years experience in resolving disputes. He is affectionately known as Action Jack because he is always happy and gets things done. www.bethestaryouare.com.

Father Patrick McGrath-Sports

Fr. Patrick McGrath was born in Ireland and was ordained a Catholic Priest in 1965. He participated actively in sports at a high school and college level and took on the development of people as a coach. As a community activist, he saw the challenges from drugs, alcohol, and gangs, and sought to do something about them. He is currently working on a memoir with co-author, Cynthia Brian titled, *I Remember.* www.bethestaryouare.com.

Anna Myers-Differences

Anna Myers is a teenager who grew up in San Francisco, a city of diversity, and has always had an appreciation for the differences among people. She also lived in China for a year. Apart from dancing, she likes anime and manga, gore movies, music from folk to metal (no country or rap please), strawberries, Star Trek, astronomy, and rats. www.bethestaryouare.com.

Erica Miner-Friends

Erica Miner, formerly a violinist with the New York Metropolitan Opera, is the author of the award-winning novel, *Travels With My Lovers,* and the new book, *FourEver Friends.* Also a screenwriter, her screenplays have won awards in recognized competitions. She is a top-rated speaker for Royal Caribbean Cruise Lines. www.ericaminer.com.

Steve Mitchell-Forgiveness

Mr. Mitchell is a former executive with the IBM Corporation, where he brought his positive approach to IBM's clients, as well as internally to the organization. Steve is an instructor for Junior Achievement and has created, directed, and hosted many philanthropic events in Northern California. A graduate of the Center for Creative Leadership, Steve resides in California with his wife, Lesley, children Alley and Brad, and Old English sheepdog, Daisy. www.bethestaryouare.com.

Justin Murray-Breathing; Serendipity

Justin Murray's passion for writing bloomed at the age of fifteen due to an offhand comment by his brother. Justin was home-schooled his entire life, prior to attending the Georgia Institute of Technology. He enjoys writing, playing the violin, singing, computer programming, and simply learning things. www.bethestaryouare.com.

Nora Catherine Nordan-Understanding

Nora Catherine Nordan divides her time between Dublin, Ireland, where she was born, and Oslo, Norway, where she now lives. Married to an economist, she has two student sons. She is Director of Studies at Treider, Norway's oldest private independent College of Commerce. Nora and co-author Cynthia Brian have been pen pals, corresponding first by letter, and now increasingly by e-mail, since their pre-teen convent school days on opposite sides of the Atlantic. www.bethestaryouare.com.

Sujin Park-Leadership

Sujin Park was born in Korea, lived in Great Britain, and has been in California since her sophomore year in high school. She has volunteered since her arrival in America at Be the Star You Are! charity where she is the Teen Chairperson. Sujin enjoys listening to music, traveling, and snowboarding. She has also gained an interest in reading since she has been working with Be the Star You Are! Charity. Through her numerous responsibilities, she learned to be an effective leader and organizer. She is excited to have been accepted at New York University, NYU. www.bethestaryouare.org.

Neha Patel-Appreciation

Diagnosed with depression, schizophrenia, and obsessive-compulsive disorder at sixteen, Neha read stories from Cynthia Brian's book, *Be the Star You Are! 99 Gifts for Living, Loving, Laughing, and Learning to Make a Difference* to augment medical treatments and therapy. "Despite the hardships I've faced, it's the people who have made a difference in my outlook on life. I encourage everyone to be optimistic and be happy," writes Neha. While searching on-line for volunteer opportunities in 2009, she was ecstatic to discover Be the Star You Are! charity. Never in her wildest dreams did she imagine the letter of appreciation she wrote would be included in a book. www.bethestaryouare.org.

M.J. Ryan-Happiness

M. J. Ryan is one of creators of the *Random Acts of Kindness* series and the author of *This Year I Will...How to Finally Change a Habit, Keep a Resolution or Make a Dream Come True; Attitudes of Gratitude; The Power of Patience; The Happiness Makeover;* and many other titles. www.mj-ryan.com

Dr. Bernie Siegel-Success; Survival

Dr. Bernie Siegel has touched many lives all over our planet through his numerous books, tapes, presentations, and Exceptional Cancer Patient therapies. In 1978 he began talking about patient empowerment and the choice to live fully and die in peace. His best selling books include *Love. Medicine & Miracles* (1986), *Peace, Love & Healing* (1989), *How To Live Between Office Visits* (1993), *Prescriptions for Living* (1998) plus many more. In 2004 he released his first book for children, *Smudge Bunny*, followed by *Love, Magic, and Mud Pies* and 2008's *Buddy's Candle.* His newest book is *Faith, Hope, and Healing.* As a physician, who has cared for and counseled innumerable people whose mortality has been threatened by an illness, Bernie embraces a philosophy of living and dying that stands at the forefront of the medical ethics and spiritual issues our society grapples with today. Dr. Siegel wrote the foreword for Cynthia Brian's debut book, *Be the Star You Are!* He continues to assist in the breaking of new ground in the field of healing while spreading the message of kindness and love. www.BernieSiegelMD.com.

Pat Stone-Letting Go

Pat Stone is the publisher and editor of *GreenPrints, The Weeder's Digest,* the heartwarming, humorous, and utterly inspiring magazine that shares the personal side of gardening. One reader called it "a hyacinth for the soul." He has four wonderful (if grown) children and the kindest wife in life. Pat co-authored the *New York Times* best seller, *Chicken Soup for the Gardener's Soul.* Visit www.greenprints.com.

Arlyn Van Dyke-Healing

Arlyn Van Dyke's roots are in a small country town in northwest Iowa where he grew up as one of five children on a farm. After his shotgun accident, he spent four years at the University of Iowa, earning degrees in science and physical therapy. He has lived and worked in Colorado and northern California. With his wonderful wife and beautiful daughter, he has lived a very full and enriching life practicing the gift of healing. www.bethestaryouare.com.

Danielle Wong-Faith

Danielle Wong (Dani) is a sixteen-year-old high school junior who enjoys spending time with family and friends. Dani is the volunteer Teen Office Assistant Chairperson with Be the Star You Are! and loves sports, photography, and traveling around the world. Writing has always been her passion because of the ability of words to have a strong impression on the reader. Dani wants to make a positive difference in the world and hopes her story impacts you to have faith. Visit www.bethestaryouare.org.

Dallas Woodburn-Writing

Dallas Woodburn, a college student at the University of Southern California, is the author of two story collections, one novel, and seventeen diaries. Her other publication credits include *Family Circle, The Writer, Writer's Digest, Cicada,* and *Justine* magazines; *The Los Angeles Times*; and six *Chicken Soup for the Soul* books. Visit www.zest.net/writeon and her blog http://dallaswoodburn.blogspot.com.

BE THE STAR YOU ARE!

empowering youth at-risk through literacy and positive media

OVERVIEW
BE THE STAR YOU ARE! 501, C3

Proceeds from sales of ***Be the Star You Are! for TEENS***
benefit Be the Star You Are! 501 c3

THE FIGHT AGAINST ILLITERACY

"To be a leader, you must be a reader."
Cynthia Brian, Founder and Executive Director

The cost of illiteracy to American taxpayers and businesses is $25 billion dollars per year. Illiteracy is a growing epidemic causing irreparable damage to our society. Low literacy and communication skills have been identified in studies as major contributors to general conduct disorders, psychiatric disorders, criminal behavior, and adolescent suicide. (Department of Communications and Public Affairs, March 12, 2001).

According to the Education Portal Report of 2007, forty-four million adults in the United States are illiterate and each year that number increases by two and a half million people. Fifty million American adults are limited to a fourth or fifth grade reading level. Between forty-six and fifty-one percent of American adults are below the individual threshold of poverty because of their inability to read. Last year, nearly four in ten fourth-graders nationwide failed to achieve even partial mastery of the reading skills needed for school success. In our highest-poverty schools, nearly seven in 10 fourth-graders fail to read at this basic level. (National Institute for Literacy) To determine how many prison beds will be needed in future years, many states base their projections on how well current elementary students perform on reading tests. Stronger literacy skills are in order for all Americans to take full advantage of continuing lifelong learning opportunities.

Of the one billion illiterate people in the world, two-thirds are women. On average, illiterate women bear six to eight children compared with literate women who have two. Infant mortality is reduced by 20% when a woman has four to six years of elementary education. As the education level of adults improves, so does their children's success in school. Helping low-literate adults improve their basic skills has a direct and measurable impact on both the education and quality of life of their children. The following statistics are for the United States based on research completed in 2008:

★ 46-51% of people with the lowest literacy skills live in poverty.
★ 50% of adults cannot read a book written at an eighth grade level.
★ 20% of Americans are functionally illiterate.
★ 17% of people with the lowest literacy skills receive food stamps
★ 70% of people with the lowest literacy skills have no full or part time job.
★ 75% of unemployed adults are illiterate.
★ 75% of employed adults have difficulty reading and/or writing.
★ 75% of those on welfare cannot read.
★ 60% of American prison inmates are illiterate.
★ 85% of juvenile offenders have difficulties reading.
★ 75% of Fortune 500 companies provide some level of remedial training for an estimated eight million workers at an estimated cost of $300 million per year.

The number one reason cited for illiteracy is a lack of access to books. To live and prosper in this society, all people must be empowered with self-esteem, become lifelong learners with access to knowledge and skills that can sustain our lives at work, at home, and in our communities.

MISSION

Be the Star You Are! is a not-for-profit 501(c)(3) corporation whose mission is to empower women, families, and youth through improved literacy and positive media.

Be the Star You Are! collects, distributes, and promotes books and other positive media to women, families, and youth at risk as a way to increase literacy, decrease violence, raise life skills, self worth, and self esteem. This media ranges from education and advisement to inspiration and guidance and covers every aspect of life, from abuse through money management.

Be the Star You Are! promotes the creed, "Read, Lead, Succeed!"

Be the Star You Are! saves trees through its book recycling programs by rescuing and redistributing many of the millions of unsold or damaged books that are shredded and burned each year. Being a conscientious steward of the earth is important to the organization.

PROGRAMS

Be the Star You Are! offers a number of focused literacy and empowerment programs including **Be the Star You Are!** radio program which is syndicated and podcast in several markets around the world showcasing experts, authors, and selected books to encourage literacy, self-worth, and a positive life style. The official radio station of the charity is World Talk Radio/Voice America. (http://www.bethestaryouareradio.com) Through the **Be the Star You Are!** Amazon bookstore, the charity offers books from interviewed authors at the least expensive price possible. Reading SPELLS Success is the audio book program whereby volunteer voice actors read children's books for podcasts. In addition, **Be the Star You Are!** employs a volunteer Star Teen Book Review Team that read and review books for children and teens. These reviews are published at *The Reading Tub* to aid parents, teachers, and librarians in making informed decisions on what books will entertain and educate children and teens. The annual National Essay Contest offers aspiring writers an opportunity to get published and to express their ideas to a global community through a radio interview. Paint-a-pot and plant-a-seed (a metaphor for planting the seeds of literacy) is a signature outreach project for kids utilized at community events by volunteers. The StarSearcher's Express newsletter is sent monthly to over 81,000 subscribers with news, inspirational quotes, tips, and spotlight on the volunteers.

Be the Star You Are! also mobilizes for disaster relief shipping thousands of books, media, videos, and other resources under its "Operation" series of programs. To date, families who were victims of 9/11 were assisted through Operation Ground Hero, Hurricane Katrina and Rita victims received aid through Operation Hurricane Relief, and children who lost their homes in the Southern California fires received holiday books with Operation Fire Relief.

Be the Star You Are! is a volunteer organization that operates through contributions, in-kind donations, and proceeds from fund-raising events. **Be the Star You Are!** does not receive state or federal funding and is solely dependent on contributions from the community and corporations.

Be the Star You Are! supports all ethnicity's and has no religious or political agendas or affiliations.

Be the Star You Are!® is a registered trademark.

DECREASING VIOLENCE

The prevalence of violence in the media and its potential harm is a concern for many family and community members. Today's youth are finding it increasingly difficult to recognize that they have the ability, responsibility, and power to determine their own destiny and choose their own future. To help them, they need access to positive and productive information and role models that will lead them beyond the negative messages in the media, and on to becoming the individual stars that they are. Everyone needs to discover passion, learn life skills, gain effective conflict management skills, and build self-esteem. Be the Star You Are! believes this can be accomplished through improving literacy and positive messages for women, families, and kids.

STATISTICS

The American Psychiatric Association reported that by the time a child turns eighteen, he or she will have witnessed 200,000 acts of violence and 16,000 simulated murders in the media. The National Crime Victimization Survey (NCVS) reported that juveniles under age eighteen were involved in 27% of all serious violent victimizations, including 14% of sexual assaults, 30% of robberies, and 27% of aggravated assaults. A Joint Statement on the Impact of Entertainment Violence on Children issued by numerous medical and psychiatric organizations stated, "entertainment violence can lead to increases in aggressive attitudes, values, and behavior, particularly in children." Research concerning violence in the media points "overwhelming to a causal connection between media violence and aggressive behavior in children."

Today's kids may be more computer literate than teens twenty-years ago, but are youth of the 21st century more *literate*? The answer to this question is no, according to a report by the National Endowment of the Arts (NEA) in November 2007.

America's youth are reading significantly less than they did twenty years ago. The NEA's report, *To Read or Not to Read* states that only one-third of thirteen-year-olds read for pleasure and that 50% of Americans age 18-24 read no books at all. Reading among adolescents thirteen years of age has declined five percent since 1984 and by ten percent among seventeen-year-old Americans. While 31% of seventeen-year-olds reported reading every day in 1984, only 22% of these adolescents read every day in 2004. Children ages 6-17 only spend one hour and forty-three minutes per day reading while they spend seven to fourteen hours a day watching television. Furthermore, 20% of the reading time is also spent engaging in other forms of media, such as playing video games or surfing the Internet. Of the top seventy best selling video games, 89% portrayed some type of violence, and 17% boasted violence as their primary focus. Adults watch an average of seven hours of television daily, with 40% reporting that they'll watch "whatever is on". The United States Department of Education reports that before the average child enters kindergarten more than 5,000 hours of TV viewing has incurred. It takes less time to earn a Bachelor's degree!

American families are spending less time and money on books than at any other time in the past two decades. As Americans read less, their reading and comprehension skills worsen. Children with fewer books in the household also performed more poorly in history and science test scores. Illiteracy is also the number one cause of children dropping out of school. Dropouts cost our nation $240 billion annually in social service expenditures and lost tax revenues.

Teens with poor self-esteem are more vulnerable to peer pressure, more likely to have depressive reactions, eating disorders, and low achievement standards. They are at higher risk to abuse alcohol and drugs, partake in violent activities, and to take risks such as driving dangerously.

The decline in reading is a problem existing in families. While technology and media may be implicated as a deterrent for reading, they may be able to serve as tools for increasing literacy when positive choices are provided. Of the employers surveyed, reading comprehension was ranked first as the most desirable skill for prospective employees.

Be the Star You Are! was founded in 1999 by Cynthia Brian, known as "The Renaissance Woman with Soul" whose list of achievements include author, producer, wife, mother, model, actor, coach, teacher, interior designer, gardener, casting director, television and radio host. Her belief is that we were not created equal. Each individual is unique with the potential of achieving greatness when provided the opportunity, encouragement, and direction to develop a plan, obtain the skills, go into action, and most of all, believe in themselves and all their possibilities. It was this desire to help people enhance their quality of living and experience life's joy that motivated Cynthia to found **Be the Star You Are!** as a non-profit organization devoted to empowering women, families, and youth through improved literacy and positive media. As the Executive Director, Cynthia strives to instill the credo of "Read, lead, succeed" by example, encouraging recruits to think outside the box, take measured risks, makes mistakes and understand that failure is fertilizer.

"The books received by Cheerful Givers, a nonprofit organization providing birthday gifts to children living in poverty, have truly made a difference in the lives of less fortunate children, many of whom have never owned a book. Be The Star You Are! is an extremely well-run and efficient organization whose leadership is totally dedicated to serving those most in need." Karen Kitchel, President, Cheerful Givers

POSITIVE RESULTS

As of April 2009, **Be the Star You Are!** has served approximately 199,800 individuals and families within 60 organizations and has logged more than 209,880 volunteer hours, while distributing over $1.6 million in resources. **Be the Star You Are!** radio program broadcasts to 5.5 million listeners in 82 countries. More than 1500 authors, experts, and professionals have been interviewed on our show. Over 400 books have been read and reviewed by our Star Teen Book Review Team and published by publishers, *The Reading Tub*, and on our web site at www.bethestaryouare.org

NATIONAL OUTREACH SUCCESS STORIES

1. **Operation Ground Hero**–With the attacks on America on September 11, 2001, **Be the Star You Are!** was one of the first charities to offer support and resources to the victims. Several hundred local volunteers as well as volunteers around the country helped us ship over 50 pallets of uplifting materials valued at over $57,000.

2. **Operation Hurricane Relief**–After Hurricanes Katrina and Rita in 2005, **Be the Star You Are!** partnered with volunteers in the South to deliver $27,000 worth of books and resources to libraries, schools, groups, and shelters.

3. **Operation Fire Relief**–Only four years after the devastating Cedar Fires, Southern California experienced over a dozen wildfires raging for two months from October to December of 2007. With thousands of families left homeless, **Be the Star You Are!** worked with relief agencies to deliver over $10,000 of books and holiday gifts to children.

HOW YOU CAN HELP

★ Send a tax deductible contribution
★ Offer a monetary donation in tribute or memoriam of a loved one
★ Buy quantities of our signature books directly from www.bethestaryouare.org
★ Shop for books and CD's at our Amazon Store http://www.amazon.com/shops/be_the_star_you_are_charity
★ Sponsor our Annual Essay Contest
★ Advertise in our newsletter, StarSearcher's Express
★ Donate air miles
★ Sponsor or be a guest on our syndicated radio program
★ Donate goods that can be auctioned off at an event
★ Make Be the Star You Are! the beneficiary of your United Way donation

- ★ Shop at your favorite stores on-line by visiting our on-line shops at http://www.bethestaryouare.org/Shop.html
- ★ Sponsor an event making Be the Star You Are! the charitable beneficiary
- ★ Donate through Ebay/Missionfish at http://donations.ebay.com/charity/charity.jsp?NP_ID=1504
- ★ Ask your company to match your donation or make a contribution
- ★ Volunteer time
- ★ Become a Benefactor
- ★ Establish A Charitable Giving Account with an Investment Firm

All donations are tax deductible according to law. Contributions are utilized to expand our efforts to support women, families, youth-groups, and youth at risk. This expansion includes:

- ★ Reading SPELLS Success!
- ★ STAR teen book reviews
- ★ Creation of a youth writing program
- ★ Social networking services
- ★ Publication of ***Be the Star You Are! for TEENS***
- ★ Production of SHINE, the webisode
- ★ Training & mentoring
- ★ Teen symposium
- ★ Acquisition of resources
- ★ Distribution of resources
- ★ Community awareness
- ★ Media production
- ★ Office administration
- ★ Radio broadcasts of positive programming
- ★ *Operation Disaster Relief* programs

Be the Star You Are! consistently validates its ability to make a difference in the lives of young people by providing them with the tools and encouragement they need to achieve personal development. Be the Star You Are! receives continual accolades from the organizations with which it works and the individuals that it benefits. Be the Star You Are! has demonstrated fiscal responsibility, competent personnel, and strong support from the community.

Encouraging, inspiring, informing, motivating, and empowering women, families, and youth through increased literacy and positive media. *Everybody counts!*

The fight against illiteracy is a continuing battle. Please join our efforts by making a tax-deductible contribution today. For additional information please contact:

Be the Star You Are!® 501 c3
PO Box 376
Moraga, California 94556
Phone: 925.376.7126
http://www.bethestaryouare.org
info@bethestaryouare.org

Thank you for daring to care.

Statistics were obtained from the following sources: National Institute for Literacy, National Center for Adult Literacy, The Kaiser Foundation, The Endowment for the Arts, The United States Department of Education, The National Crime Victimization Survey, The Literacy Company, The American Psychiatric Association, The American Academy of Pediatrics, American Medical Association, American Psychological Association, American Academy of Family Physicians, American Academy of Child and Adolescent Psychiatry ,U.S. Census Bureau.

BE THE STAR
YOU ARE!

WHO IS CYNTHIA BRIAN?

Author, Speaker, TV /Radio Personality,

Spokesperson, Coach, Philanthropist

www.cynthiabrian.com

Cynthia Brian, New York Times best selling co-author of *Chicken Soup for the Gardener's Soul*, author of *Be the Star You Are! 99 Gifts for Living, Loving, Laughing, and Learning to Make a Difference, The Business of Show Business*, and *Miracle Moments,* is an internationally acclaimed key note speaker, personal growth consultant, host of radio and TV shows, syndicated columnist and acting coach. The media often refers to Cynthia as "the Renaissance Woman with Soul!" She is a world traveler who speaks French, Spanish, Italian, and Dutch. With nearly three decades of experience working in the entertainment field as an actor, model, producer, writer, coach, designer, host, and casting director, she has had the honor of performing with some of the biggest names in the industry. Cynthia is a Certified Interior Designer and has had her interior and garden design projects featured in TV, commercials, books, and numerous publications. Ms. Brian is a much in demand lecturer on luxury cruise lines and spas around the world, inspiring others to be the stars they were born to be by creating a life they design.

Because of her devotion to increasing literacy and positive messages in the world, Cynthia founded and is the Executive Director of the 501(c)(3) charity, Be the Star You Are! (www.bethestaryouare.org) empowering women, families, and youth at risk. Her motto is "To be a leader, you must be a reader!"

Ms. Brian is also dedicated to helping others achieve their dreams, with a focus on teens, by implementing their unique gifts, and has coached many aspiring thespians, writers, and professionals to fame and fortune through her personal success consultations in acting, media, writing, presentations, and life challenges. Because of her energy and passion, companies engage Cynthia's services as a media spokesperson. She is the home, garden, and lifestyle expert for Internet sites and a writer for numerous publications, including being the inspirational gardening columnist for the *Lamorinda Weekly*. She and her daughter, Heather Brittany, are known as the Stella Donne Goddess Gals, working together in films, TV, radio, writing assignments, and speaking engagements. (www.goddessgals.com)

Born on a farm in the Napa Valley in northern California, the eldest of five children, Cynthia raised chickens and sheep, drove tractors, and picked fruit to earn enough money to pay her way through college. After being honored as the Outstanding Teenager of California, she was named teenage ambassador to Holland and served as a foreign correspondent for several newspapers. Her travel expeditions gave birth to her writing, speaking, and coaching career.

Interviewing is a talent this dynamic woman enjoys. She has been dubbed "Oprah of the Airwaves." Tune into her upbeat positive nationally syndicated radio program, *Starstyle-Be the Star You Are!***,** live and archived weekly on World Talk Radio/Voice America where she interviews authors and experts during a power hour of edu-tainment. (www.starstyleradio.com)

When you are seeking a seasoned professional spokesperson for your next project—a wife, mom, and business expert with exuberance and personality that garners results, Cynthia Brian is the lady to call! Cynthia is available for private coaching, consultations, and speaking engagements.

Contact:

Starstyle® Productions, LLC
PO Box 422,
Moraga, Ca. 94556,
phone: 925-377-STAR (7827)
www.star-style.com and www.bethestaryouare.com
Cynthia@star-style.com

Former President Ronald Reagan honoring Cynthia Brian as the Outstanding Teenager of California.

WHAT'S NEXT?

Now that you have the tools to be the star you were born to be, it's time to get started implementing the principles. Are you ready to jumpstart your life and live your dreams? Read a chapter every day and get inspired to create your dynamic destiny. Coach Cynthia Brian wants to help you every step of the way. She is available to be your personal cheerleader and guide on the side. To schedule your consultation or phone session, contact Cynthia by email, Cynthia@star-style.com or call 925-377-STAR (7827). Cynthia is also available as a motivational speaker, consultant, and coach to schools, organizations, companies, and conferences around the globe. Contact Cynthia@star-style.com or call 925-377-STAR (7827).

You deserve success and happiness. Become unstoppable! The end is the beginning.

☆

FREE BONUS!

Thank you once again for purchasing ***Be the Star You Are! for TEENS***. As my gift to you for reading this book, I am offering *free* bonuses and priority discounts that will help you smile, have fun, and be wild and wacky. To claim your freebies and get your party started, register at www.bethestaryouare.com/BookBonus.html. Keep living, loving, laughing, learning, and leading, and most of all enjoy the now. You are a ***STAR!***

Register at www.bethestaryouare.com/bonusbook.html

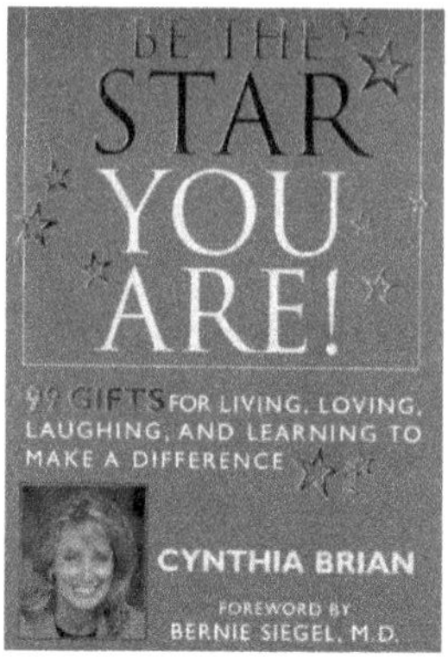

Cynthia Brian
Starstyle® Productions, LLC
PO Box 422,
Moraga, Ca. 94556,
phone: 925-377-STAR (7827)
www.star-style.com
www.bethestaryouare.com
Cynthia@star-style.com

Tune in to the internationally syndicated weekly broadcast of *Starstyle-Be the Star You Are!* hosted by "the Oprah of the Airwaves", Cynthia Brian, and co-hosted by Heather Brittany (known as the Stella Donne Goddess Gals) on World Talk Radio/ Voice America. Brought to the airwaves as a literacy outreach program of Be the Star You Are!® charity, you'll meet amazing authors with exceptional books that will enrich and enhance your life. Get ready to smile, have fun, and be wild and wacky as the Dynamic Duo help you to pump your energy, live, love, laugh, and learn to make a difference. You have a personal invitation to participate in our power party. It's time to celebrate. Join us!

Visit www.bethestaryouareradio.com or
http://www.star-style.com/radio/home.htm for schedules.

☆

ORDER FORM

Give the gift of ***Be the Star You Are! for TEENS!***

Please ask about case and quantity discounts. A variety of books, CDS, DVDS, videos, and other empowerment tools are available directly from www.star-style.com/store/index.htm.

We accept VISA, MASTERCARD, PayPal, and checks.
Phone Orders: Call 877-944-STAR or 925-377-STAR (7827)

Please send_______copies of ***Be the Star You Are! for TEENS***

Name ____

Company Name ______________________________________

Address ____

City______________________ State______________ Zip________

Phone__________________ Email___________________________

Would you like the book autographed? ____________________

If yes, please spell name legibly_______________________

Cost per book: **$17.95**
California residents, please add **10 percent** tax
Shipping: please add **$5.00 per book**

Total enclosed______________

Method of Payment

Check_____________
Credit Card VISA or MASTERCARD only

Card Number___________________________________

Expiration Date________ 3 Digit Code________ Zip code of card________

Signature____

Send to: PO Box 376, Moraga, California 94556 or email: Cynthia@bethestaryouare.org

Proceeds benefit Be the Star You Are!® 501 c3 empowering women, families, and youth through improved literacy, life skills, and positive media. www.bethestaryouare.org.

Thank you for purchasing our book and keep being the star you are!

All prices are subject to change and are current at time of publication.

Printed in the USA
CPSIA information can be obtained
at www.ICGtesting.com
JSHW082154140824
68134JS00014B/240

9 781600 376320